The Making of ST. PETERSBURG

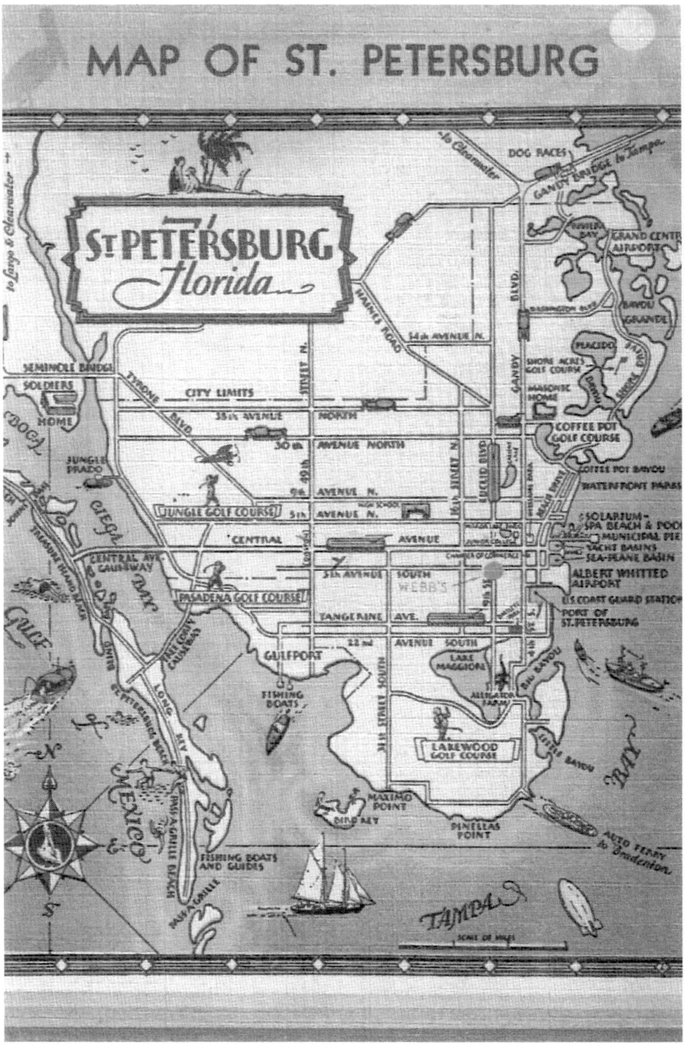

Map of mid-century St. Petersburg. *Courtesy of Michaels Family Collection.*

The Making of ST. PETERSBURG

WILL MICHAELS

THE History PRESS

Published by The History Press
Charleston, SC 29403
www.historypress.net

Cover image of Babe Ruth courtesy of Linda Ruth Tosetti.

First published 2012
Sedcond printing 2015
Updated 2026

Manufactured in the United States

ISBN 978.1.60949.833.7

Library of Congress Cataloging-in-Publication Data

Michaels, Will.
The making of St. Petersburg / Will Michaels.
pages cm
Includes bibliographical references and index.
ISBN 978-1-60949-833-7
1. Saint Petersburg (Fla.)--History. 2. Saint Petersburg (Fla.)--Social life and customs. 3. Historic buildings--Florida--Saint Petersburg. 4. Saint Petersburg (Fla.)--Buildings, structures, etc. 5. Saint Petersburg (Fla.)--Biography. I. Title. II. Title: Making of Saint Petersburg.
F319.S24M53 2012
975.9'63--dc23
2012044159

For my love
Kathy

My children
Laura, Mark and Jeannie

And my grandchildren
Mariel, William, Lynne and Michael

Contents

Foreword

Will Michaels is a St. Petersburg treasure. For many years, the city's residents have appreciated his articles in the *Northeast Journal*. His writings range from telling the stories of local celebrities such as William Straub and Katherine Bell Tippetts to the development of the Old Northeast and Snell Isle neighborhoods and the history of St. Petersburg's entertainment centers. His interests begin with the community's early years, ranging from its nineteenth-century origins to the coming of the Orange Belt Railway in 1888, the first major league spring training baseball games at Coffee Pot Bayou and the launching of the world's first commercial airline in 1914. He has written about myriad topics, both historical and biographical, including "Christmas of Yesteryears," some of the city's most influential (and bizarre!) leaders and several fascinating presidential election campaigns in St. Petersburg and Pinellas County.

Michaels writes with the measured eye of an anthropologist (he has a doctorate in the subject) and the soul of a resident who clearly adores his city. But he is not an unabashed booster. His articles reveal warts and imperfections in our city in addition to the city's famous waterfront parks and iconic green benches. His many contributions to the community include the directorship of the St. Petersburg Museum of History and a term as president of the Council of Neighborhood Associations (CONA). He has also been a passionate leader in historic preservation, both as a member and president of St. Petersburg Preservation (SPP). For several years he taught a popular course on St. Petersburg history at St. Petersburg College. Now, with the publication of this rich collection of his best articles, he shares his understanding of St. Petersburg's distinctive history and culture with a wider audience. Surely, *The Making of St. Petersburg* will burnish his reputation as a devoted and valued citizen of his adopted hometown.

Gary R. Mormino
Frank E. Duckwall Professor of Florida History
University of South Florida St. Petersburg

Raymond Arsenault
John Hope Franklin Professor of Southern History
University of South Florida St. Petersburg

Preface

This is a selection of articles previously published by the St. Petersburg *Northeast Journal* between 2004 and 2012. The articles cover various aspects of the history of St. Petersburg and Pinellas County and are roughly arranged in chronological order. They were selected to give both an overview of key events and notable personalities of our history and to provide a general "sense of place" for our city. The articles have been lightly edited to make them current and, to some extent, link them together, and they are presented as chapters. These chapters are also grounded in my local history course previously offered through the Life Long Learning Program at St. Petersburg College. The course was entitled "Turning Points in St. Petersburg History." While it is recognized that there are often many antecedents to a particular event in history, and that these antecedents build up over time, nevertheless there are events that serve as benchmarks in the evolution of history at all levels.

Several chapters have special significance as they deal with three centennial events. One is the centennial of the creation of Pinellas County in 2012. Two other centennials will be celebrated in 2014. The first of these is the launching of the world's first airline, which occurred on January 1, 1914. The second is the beginning of Major League Baseball's spring training, which began with the St. Louis Browns on February 16, 1914. Both were momentous events. The first marked the beginning of a new cutting-edge technology that has since transformed the world. The second was the beginning of a love affair between Major League Baseball and St. Petersburg that left an enduring stamp on our city's sense of place.

History is a cumulative affair. As years pass, we usually obtain a fuller and more complete understanding of earlier events. Sometimes this is the result of new information, sometimes the result of new perspectives. Much of the material in this book is derived from previous local histories. These particularly include such major works as Karl H. Grismer's *The Story of St. Petersburg* (1948), Walter P. Fuller's *St. Petersburg and Its People* (1972) and Raymond Arsenault's *St. Petersburg and the Florida Dream: 1888–1950* (1988). Dr. Arsenault's work still remains the "Bible" of our local history, and his insights and keen observations are frequently quoted in this effort. Rosalie Peck and Jon Wilson's works have been relied on especially to access the history of our African American community. I would be remiss if I did not also mention the work of my friend the late Scott Taylor Hartzell. Scott in particular made an important contribution to oral history and local biography.

Many other works of local history and city documents have been drawn upon, as well as oral histories taken by the St. Petersburg Museum of History's Founding Families Project, which I have had the privilege to participate in since its beginning in 2008. This work is intended to be a selective history, addressing only a sampling of our city's turning points and highlights, with an emphasis on our city's sense of place. The topics selected are generally covered more fully than in previous histories. For those wishing to read a detailed comprehensive history, I highly recommend Dr. Arsenault's authoritative and very readable work.

The title of this work is *The Making of St. Petersburg*, and the first chapter describing the origins of our city also uses that title. As cities are made and evolve, they develop a sense of place, and that is the thread used to weave this work together. The National Trust for Historic Preservation defines "sense of place" as: "Those things that add up to a feeling that a community is a special place, distinct from anywhere else." Such special places have strong identities and characters that are deeply felt by residents and many visitors. These special places also contribute to the personal identity of those who grow up in them. The final chapter directly addresses St. Petersburg's sense of place. The chapter is based on a talk given at a panel with Ray Arsenault and Gary Mormino sponsored by St. Petersburg Preservation in 2009. The talk was later rewritten as an article published in the *Northeast Journal*.

There are actually many *senses* of place for a community. This work is by no means definitive and only suggests some of the special features typically ascribed to our city. The term "sense of place" as used here is not limited to landscape, waterscape, climate and the built environment (which may be referred to collectively simply as "landscape") but rather also encompasses the people who have lived here and made St. Petersburg their permanent home. A city's sense of place will be somewhat different for those who have lived in that place and for those who visit. For those who are visiting, our sense of place largely has to do with the physical landscape and their impressions of our people. For those who live here, sense of place includes this, but it also includes the many personal memories, social relationships and emotional meanings associated with our physical landscape. This is sometimes referred to as "social landscape." Visitors and tourists do, at times, appreciate aspects of the physical landscape that are not appreciated by the native. On the other hand, some physical landscapes have little appeal to the visitor or tourist because they have no personal associations with them. For everyone, though, knowing something of the history of St. Petersburg will add to an understanding and appreciation of our sense of place.

I wish to acknowledge the many people who have helped in one way or another with this work, including the staff at the St. Petersburg Museum of History, especially Ann Wikoff and Marta Jones; the staff at the *Northeast Journal*, particularly Jen MacMillen, Susan Woods Alderson and Julie L. Johnston; my wife, Kathy Michaels, for her encouragement and assistance with editing; and the following persons for reviewing selected chapters or aspects: Dr. Raymond Arsenault; Dr. Warren Brown; Bob Guckenberger; Jessie Marshall; Jeff Moates, MA, RPA; Dr. Gary Mormino; Dr. William Parsons; Tom Pavluvick; Linda Ruth Tosetti (granddaughter of Babe Ruth); Jon Wilson; and Fritz Wilder. Most especially I am thankful to the many people of St. Petersburg who shared their personal histories through interviews, family papers and photos.

The Making of St. Petersburg

It was a Russian by the name of Peter Demens who with General John C. Williams and his wife, Sarah, created the city of St. Petersburg. Peter Demens (pronounced de-*mens*) was a Russian aristocrat who had served as a captain in the tsar's Jaeger regiment. Despite his service in the tsar's regiment, he became an advocate for social reform. After the assassination of Tsar Alexander II and the repression that followed, he fled Russia for the United States. Another possible reason for his immigration to America may have been entanglement in some legal difficulty of which he was later acquitted. He Anglicized his name from Pyotr Alexeyevich Dementyev to Peter Demens. He soon became owner of a sawmill in Longwood, Florida, where he also was elected the town's mayor. In 1885, he signed a contract to supply railroad ties to the Orange Belt Railway. The Orange Belt was being built from the lower St. Johns River to Lake Apopka. When the owners of the railway were unable to pay him for the ties, he took over the railway. He completed the link to Apopka in 1886. He then looked about for further profitable locations to extend his railroad and settled on the Pinellas Peninsula some 120 miles distant.

Hamilton Disston, heir to a vast fortune from a tool manufacturing company, became interested in Florida real estate after making a fishing trip to the state. In 1881, he bought 4 million acres from the Florida state government for twenty-five cents per acre, making him the largest landowner in the United States. Disston was particularly interested in the Pinellas Peninsula, where he had acquired 110,000 acres. He believed

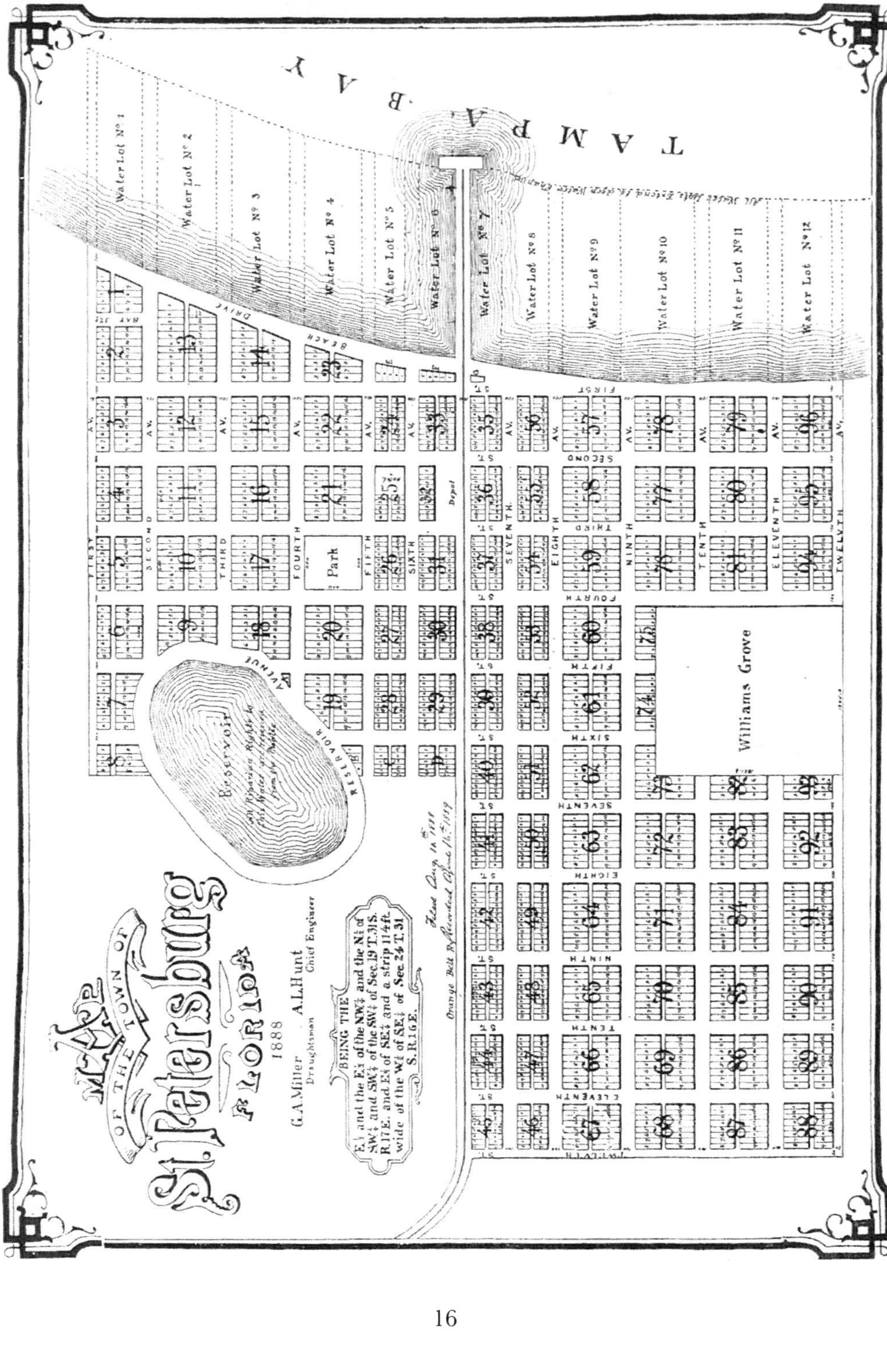
TAMPA BAY
MAP OF THE TOWN OF
St. Petersburg
FLORIDA
1888
G.A. Miller
Draughtsman
A.L. Hunt
Chief Engineer
BEING THE
E½ and the E½ of the NW¼ and the N½ of SW¼ and SW¼ of Sec. 19 T. 31S. R.17E. and E½ of SE¼ and a strip 114 ft. wide of the W¼ of SE¼ of Sec. 24 T. 31 S. R. 16E.
Reservoir
Park
Williams Grove
Depot
Orange Belt R'y

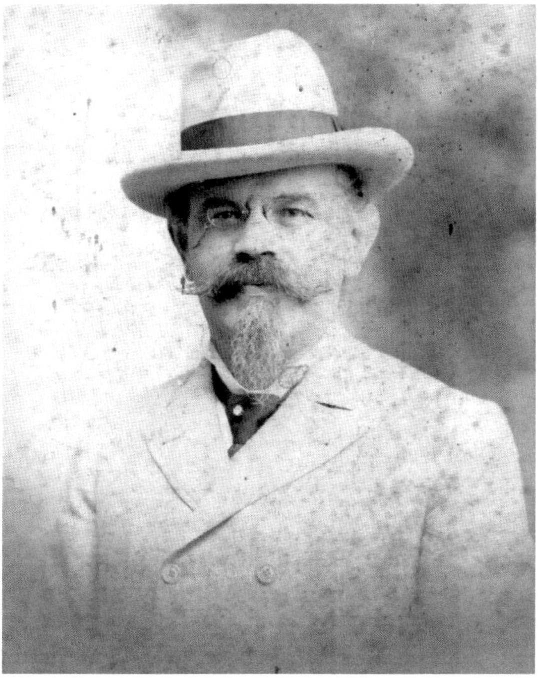

Opposite: Original town plat for St. Petersburg, dated 1888 and filed by Peter Demens in the Hillsborough County Courthouse in Tampa. Sixth Avenue later became Central Avenue. Reservoir Lake later became Mirror Lake. Williams Park is shown as "Park." It was not named in John C. Williams Sr.'s honor until after his death in 1892. *Courtesy St. Petersburg Museum of History*.

Left: Portrait of Peter Demens that at one time hung in the Detroit Hotel. In addition to bringing the railroad to the hamlet that was to become St. Petersburg, Peter Demens built the three-and-a-half-story Detroit Hotel and the three-thousand-foot-long Railroad Pier, image circa 1900. *Courtesy St. Petersburg Museum of History*.

Pinellas to be the ideal future site of a prosperous port city and consequently founded Disston City (today's Gulfport) on Boca Ciega Bay. But to really put Disston City on the map, he needed to make it the terminus of a cross-Florida railroad.

At this time, there were two railroad tsars in Florida known as the "Two Henrys": Henry Flagler and Henry Plant. Flagler's rail and companion hotel interests were confined to Florida's east coast. Plant was a self-made man who had worked as a railroad and maritime express shipping executive. After the Civil War, he acquired a network of railroads throughout the South. Plant's interests were in Central and West Florida, where he completed a railroad, the South Florida, running from Sanford to Tampa in 1884. In 1890, he completed the 511-room Tampa Bay Hotel, at the time the largest building in the world to be powered by electricity. Disston was not able to make a deal with Plant, who had invested in Tampa as Florida's major west coast city, and did not want to encourage another competing city across the bay. So Disston turned to the up-and-comer Demens. Disston offered Demens sixty thousand acres of land if Demens would rapidly extend his Orange Belt Railway to Disston City.

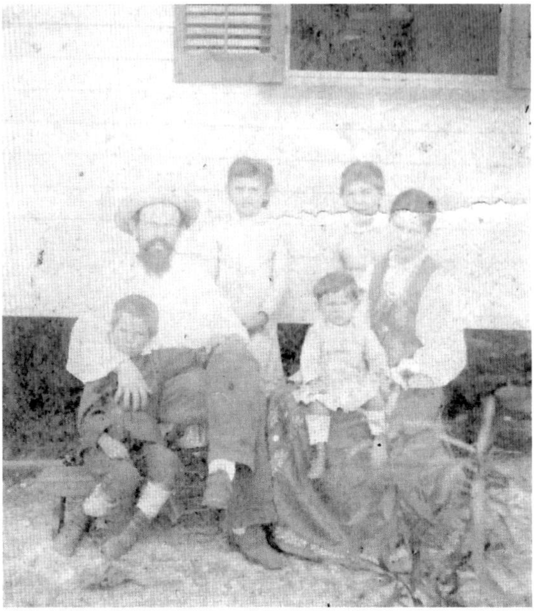

Peter Demens and his family. The photo was taken when he ran a sawmill in Longwood, image mid-1880s. *Courtesy St. Petersburg Museum of History.*

Demens, however, did not want to end his railroad at Gulfport, but instead wanted to extend it even farther to Mullet Key, which gave better access to the Gulf of Mexico. Mullet Key would later become the site of Fort De Soto. This would require expensive bridges and causeways, so he asked Disston for another fifty thousand acres to finance the extension. Disston's Florida Land and Improvement Company turned down the request.

Rebuffed, Demens looked about for an alternative site for the terminus. This was probably a calculated bluff on his part, as there was no readily apparent alternative site. At this point, Henry Sweetapple, Demens's partner, met with "General" John C. Williams and his wife, Sarah. (Williams was called "General" as a courtesy title.) Sarah Williams and Sweetapple were both Canadians, a bond that likely helped reach an agreement to bring the railroad to Williams's property, which was in the vicinity of an area then known as Paul's Landing. In exchange for diverting the railroad to this area, including the construction of a wharf deep enough to accommodate commercial shipping, Williams agreed to assign to Demens 250 acres of prime property.

Coming to an agreement was one thing, but executing it was another. The railroad extension to Pinellas was begun in January 1887. Bad weather, delayed steel shipments, defective equipment, lack of financing and even a

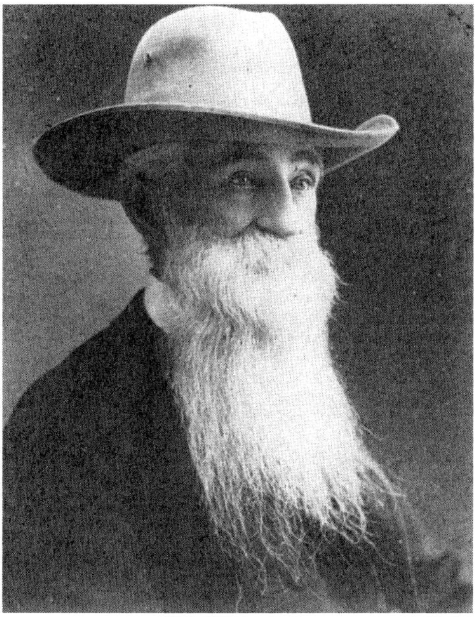

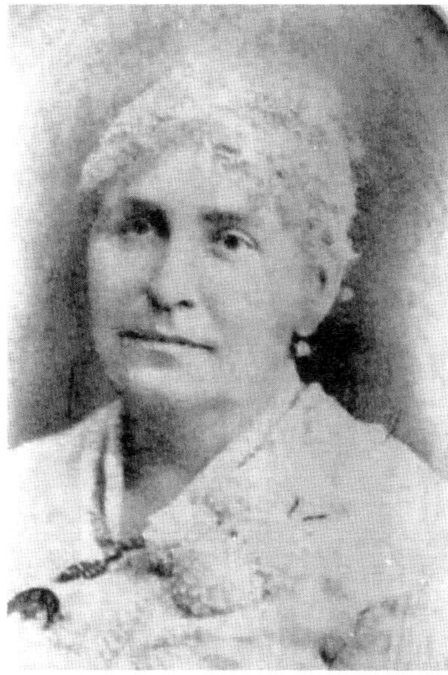

Left: General John C. Williams Sr. Williams acquired more than 1,600 acres of land in the area now known as St. Petersburg in 1875. In 1887, he signed an agreement with Peter Demens to bring the Orange Belt Railway to St. Petersburg in exchange for 250 acres of waterfront land. "General" was a courtesy title. *Courtesy Heritage Village & Library.*

Right: Sarah Williams Armistead. John Williams married a young Canadian-born widow, Sarah Craven Judge, in 1882. Sarah Williams took a lead role in negotiating the agreement to bring the Orange Belt Railway to southeast Pinellas with Peter Demens's associate, Henry Sweetapple. That Sarah Williams and Sweetapple were both Canadians probably facilitated negotiations. Sarah later married St. Petersburg mayor James Armistead after Williams's death, image circa 1907. *Courtesy St. Petersburg Museum of History.*

yellow fever epidemic challenged completion of the railroad. In September, irate creditors chained and padlocked the Orange Belt's locomotives to the rails. After witnessing this event, Henry Sweetapple died from a stroke. The padlocking was followed in October by the rail workers surrounding the Orange Belt offices and threatening to lynch Demens if they did not receive their back pay. Additionally, just as the railroad was about to reach its goal, a local property owner refused to allow the railroad to cross his land. Demens ordered tracks to be laid on either side of this property and then, in the early hours of a Sunday morning, had the tracks laid across the forbidden land before he could be stopped.

Demens and the Orange Belt Railway employed many African Americans to build the railway and the Railroad Pier. They also built

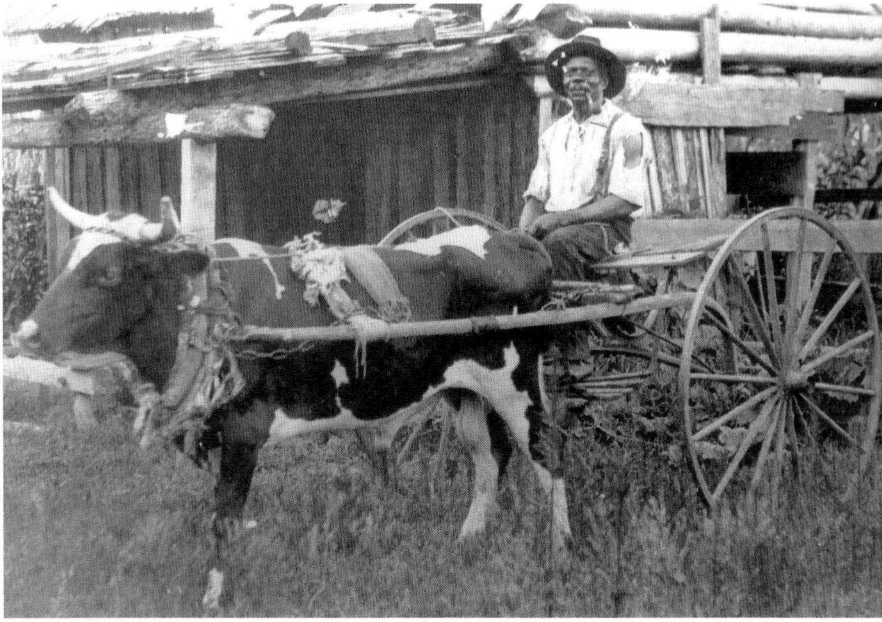

John and Anna Donaldson and their family were among the first African Americans known to settle in lower Pinellas County after the Civil War. He owned a forty-acre farm northwest of Lake Maggiore and worked on construction of the Detroit Hotel and the Railroad Pier. Donaldson is buried at the Glen Oak Cemetery in South St. Petersburg, image circa 1900. *Courtesy St. Petersburg Museum of History.*

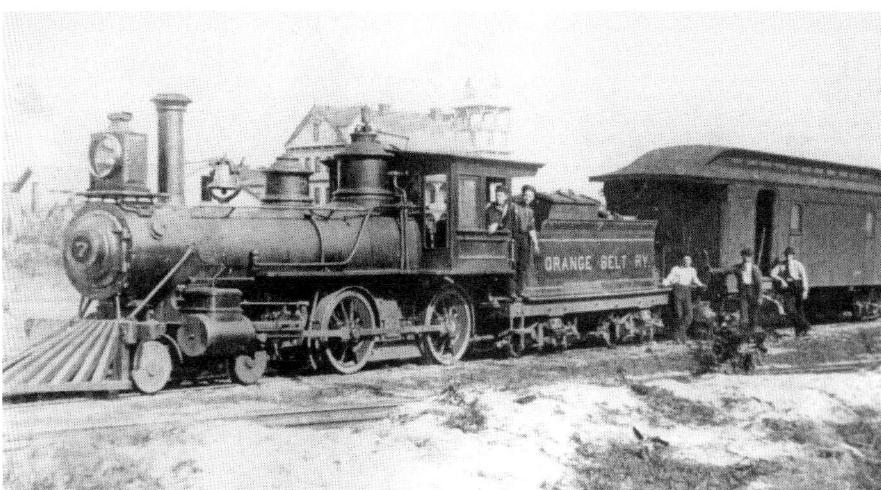

An Orange Belt train, with the Detroit Hotel in the background. St. Petersburg's founders had high hopes for an area largely populated with scrub pine and palmetto bushes, image circa 1893. *Courtesy St. Petersburg Museum of History.*

the Detroit Hotel and were its first occupants. African Americans would continue to have a major role in literally building the city and contributing to its success throughout its history.

Finally, on June 8, 1888, the locomotive Mattie puffed and huffed its way to the end of the line at what is now Ninth Street. The area was then informally known as Wardsville, but not for long. As the railroad was being built, post offices were designated at stops along the way. Ella Ward was designated the postmistress for the final stop in Wardsville. Many cities have their origin myths, and St. Petersburg is no exception. It is often told that the city and the Detroit Hotel were named as the result of a coin toss, or drawing of straws, between Williams and Demens. The winner would get to name the city and the loser the hotel.

Two other accounts are less dramatic. According to Demens's associate Joseph Henschen, as reported by historian Karl Grismer, a little before completion of the railroad Ward had gone to the Orange Belt headquarters near Lake Apopka to discuss the official name for the post office. Demens was not there at the time, but she discussed the naming with Henschen. Ward told Henschen that General Williams suggested that the city be named after one of the original backers of the Orange Belt Railway—Demens, Henschen, Sweetapple or Taylor. Henschen noted that a town had already been named after Taylor. "And we couldn't call a town Sweetapple very well—it would be doomed from the start. And my name, Henschen, wouldn't be good because no one could spell it." He then noted that Demens wanted a town to be called St. Petersburg, after Demens's prior home in Russia. But Grismer also noted that Demens had written a letter long before Demens met Williams in which he actually referred to the new town as "St. Petersburgh." It is likely this was Demens's intention all along and that Henschen's version is an understatement of a decision that had already been made. Perhaps new information will be discovered, shedding additional light on the naming of our city. The new hotel, on the other hand, was named after General Williams's hometown, Detroit.

Demens and General Williams collaborated in an ambitious town plan that called for streets one hundred feet wide and a large central park, now Williams Park. Demens also built a Russian-style railroad depot and the forty-room, three-and-a-half-story Detroit Hotel at his and the railroad's expense. The spectacle of a three-story hotel rising from the palmetto bushes and slash pines with hardly any other habitations in sight must have been a sight to behold, as well as a testament to the builders' faith in their enterprise. As historian Rita Gould described it, St. Petersburg was then "out near the back of beyond."

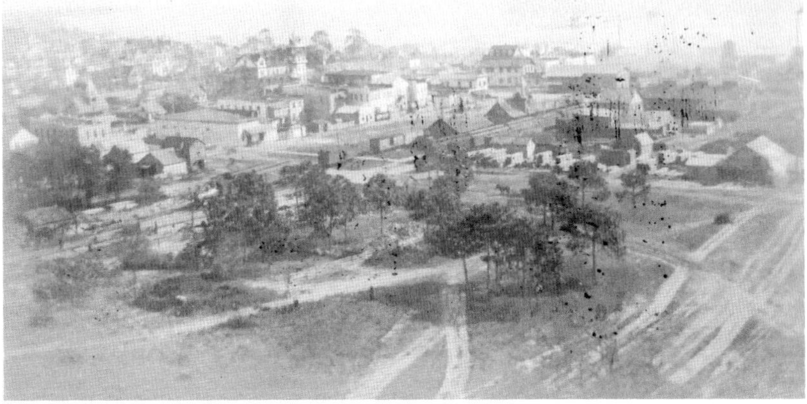

Elevated 1901 view of St. Petersburg taken from a 137-foot tower built by the city's first major philanthropist, Edwin H. Tomlinson. Tomlinson was an acquaintance of Guglielmo Marconi, inventor of the wireless telegraph. The tower was built with the expectation that Marconi would come to St. Petersburg to conduct experiments. Unfortunately, the tower was destroyed by lightning six months after it was built. Note the Detroit Hotel in the upper left and the Orange Belt Railway in the foreground, image 1901. *Courtesy St. Petersburg Museum of History.*

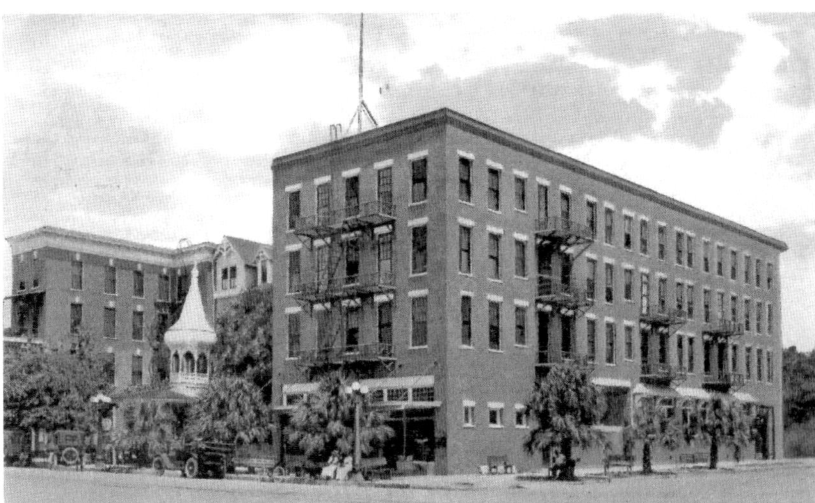

The Detroit Hotel as it still appears today. Brick vernacular wings were added between 1910 and 1914. For many years, the Detroit was the cultural center of the city. Some of its notable guests included William Jennings Bryan, Will Rogers, Clarence Darrow, Babe Ruth and John F. Kennedy. *Courtesy Michaels Family Collection.*

Despite the building of the depot and hotel, Williams refused to grant the railroad its half of the town site until the Railroad Pier was complete. The three-thousand-foot Railroad Pier was finally completed in February 1889. Not much in the way of contemporary accounts of the city's founding remain. But one small notice has been found from the *Tampa Tribune* of January 1889 regarding Williams:

> *John C. Williams Sr, the present life and soul of Pinellas Point put in an appearance a few days ago* [in Tampa], *and has been quite busy since feeding the hungry and employing the idle. Lest it were my business I could not tell you the half of the great achievements, the broad views, the liberal policies and boundless faith of this "ex-cussed" but now lauded old gentleman. His money flows like water, his charity, generosity and patriotism is limited only by his means.*

What was meant by "ex-cussed" remains an enigma we can only guess at. But one thing we do know is that he was a hard bargainer when it came to Peter Demens.

Although the Orange Belt was the largest narrow-gauge railway in the nation, it was also one of the most poorly constructed. An early visitor from Iowa described his experience: "The engine used to jump the track about once a week but I never heard of anyone being killed or even seriously injured—the train didn't go fast enough. Wood was used as fuel and in wet weather, when the wood got wet, you could keep up with the train by walking." At times, passengers had to get out and chop wood to keep it going. Historian Karl Grismer described the Orange Belt as a "comic strip railroad." Even after its sale to others, there was little improvement. In 1906, St. Petersburg's postmaster complained that only one train had arrived as little as fifty minutes late, and that was "an unusual record."

Despite the importance of the railroad to St. Petersburg, it would be a long time before it was profitable. Heavily in debt, Demens sold the railroad for $25,250 (somewhat over $600,000 in current dollars) to a syndicate of investors in 1889. The syndicate renamed the railroad the Sanford and St. Petersburg Railway in 1893. In 1895, the railroad was leased to Henry Plant. After the death of Plant in 1902, the Atlantic Coast Line absorbed the railroad. In 1913, the first special train for winter visitors arrived, carrying about 200 people. In 1914, a second railroad, the Tampa and Gulf Coast (known as "Tug and Grunt") began to provide service to St. Petersburg and linked the city with Tampa for the first time by a rather circuitous sixty-four-

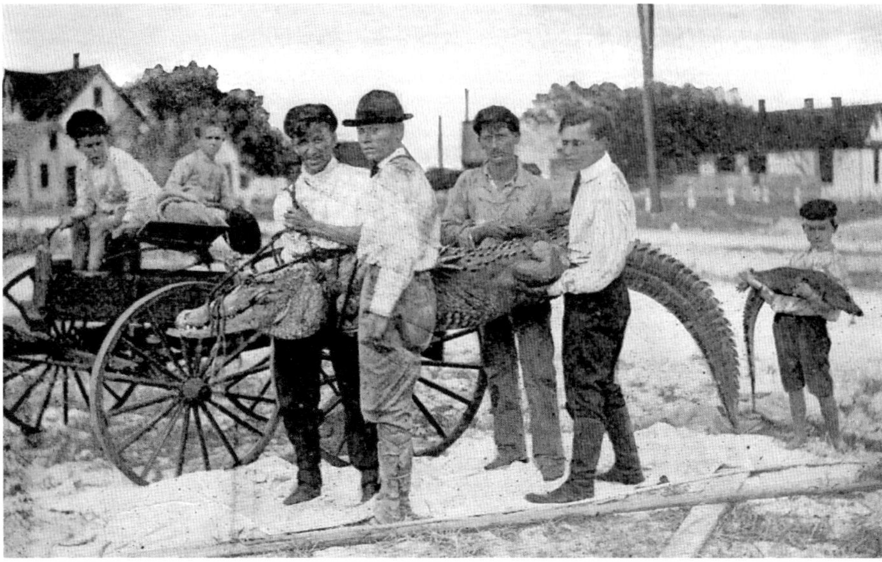

Early postcard depicts some of the adventure of living in St. Petersburg shortly after the turn of the last century. Bird Latham, manager of the St. Petersburg Electric Light & Power Company and the Trolley Company, is holding the alligator's snout. Latham later learned to fly from Tony Jannus. St. Petersburg Post Card Association, image circa 1908. *Courtesy Michaels Family Collection.*

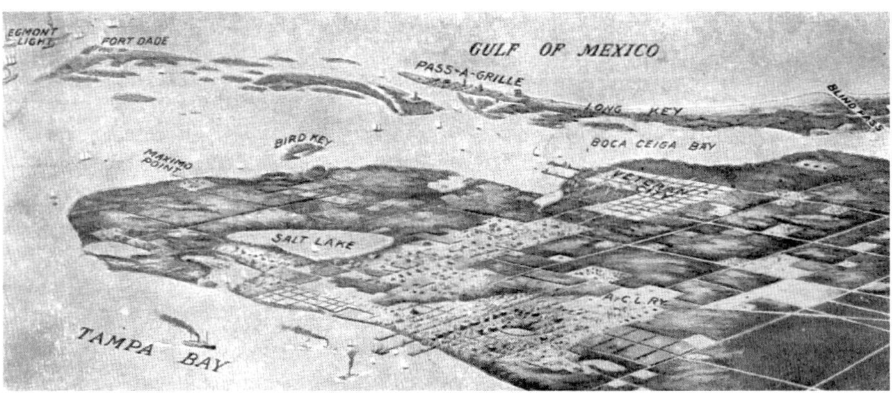

Early 1909 postcard map imagining St. Petersburg and surrounding areas. "A.C.L. RY" is the Atlantic Coastline Railway, successor to the Orange Belt Railway. Fort Dade is shown erroneously; it was located on Egmont Key. The area labeled "Fort Dade" was actually Fort De Soto on Mullet Key. Salt Lake became Lake Maggiore. Veteran City was originally Disston City. *Courtesy Michaels Family Collection.*

mile route. The trip took twelve hours. A train carrying 1,500 people to the city marked the inauguration of this line. After this event, special train promotions for tourists became frequent.

More than any single event, it was the coming of the Orange Belt Railway in 1888 that sparked the development of St. Petersburg as a new commercial and residential center. By one account, there was only one passenger on the Mattie when it first arrived in St. Pete, and this was a traveling shoe salesman who quickly left after finding few buyers for his wares. It took a while for the railroad to register its impact, but make a difference it did. Commercial fishing was at this time the most important economic activity. Traditionally, fish were sold through Tampa. But with the coming of the railroad to St. Petersburg, huge quantities of mackerel and snapper were sent by rail, packed in ice, to eastern markets. Along with the early town founders and builders, the railroad itself sought to promote tourism, including the building of a large bathing pavilion attached to the Railroad Pier. The first tourists actually came in the summer from inland Florida. Because it was surrounded by water, St. Petersburg was cooler than inland parts of the state. But the importance of tourism to the local economy was not to take hold for a few years yet. Winter tourists did not begin to arrive until the late 1890s, when much-needed improvements in rail service were finally made.

The Orange Belt gave St. Petersburg a rail tie-in with the rest of the nation. The pioneer wagon road requiring a day's travel to reach Tampa fell into disuse. Shipping and trading activity shifted away from Disston City and Pinellas Village to the new rail terminus. As historian Lynne Brown wrote, Disston City "effectively died" in 1888 when the railroad reached St. Pete. New settlers came to St. Pete, increasing the local population from less than 50 to 273. Some African Americans who worked on the railroad stayed and found work in the new town. They initially settled in an area known as Pepper Town (named for the peppers grown in the gardens) near what is today Fourth Avenue South and east of Dr. Martin Luther King Jr. Street (formerly Ninth Street).

As historian Walter P. Fuller wrote, Peter Demens and his associates may not have made money from the Orange Belt, but "[t]hey were creators. They were pioneers. They were doers…They were rich, even if their neighbors never knew it." Also included in these early pioneers are John and Sarah Williams, the laborers who built the railroad and the first hotel, as well as many others who began the making of a new city in the Pinellas subtropical wilderness.

Sources used in this chapter include Raymond Arsenault, *St. Petersburg and the Florida Dream*; Lynne Brown, *Gulfport: A Definitive History*; Walter P. Fuller, *St. Petersburg and Its People*; Karl H. Grismer, *History of St. Petersburg*; Scott Taylor Hartzell, *Voices of America: St. Petersburg, an Oral History*; Will Michaels, "The Railroad Crosses the Bay," *Northeast Journal*, 2005; Albert Parry, *Full Steam Ahead!*; Rosalie Peck and Jon Wilson, *St. Petersburg's Historic African American Neighborhoods*; George W. Pettengill, *The Story of the Florida Railroads*; Kelly Reynolds, *Henry Plant: Pioneer Empire Builder*; and Gregg M. Turner and Seth H. Bramson, *The Plant System of Railroads, Steamships, and Hotels*.

The Spanish Invasion at Boca Ciega Bay

Most authorities are in agreement that the Spanish conquistador Pánfilo de Narváez landed on the western Pinellas Peninsula, probably Boca Ciega Bay, on either April 14 or 15, 1528. He is the first known European to visit the interior of the Pinellas Peninsula, including the vicinity of present-day St. Petersburg. He is not the first documented European to explore Florida. Ponce de Leon predated him by nine years. Ponce de Leon is known to have reached the west coast of Florida, but not as far north as Tampa Bay. Narváez was also predated in reaching the larger Florida area by several other Spanish explorers. Diego Miruleo probably sailed in to Tampa Bay in 1516. Alonzo Álvarez de Pineda sailed the entire Gulf Coast in 1519 and provided the first map of the coastline of the entire Gulf of Mexico, including Tampa Bay.

By the time Narváez reached Boca Ciega Bay, he was an old hand at exploration and conquest in the New World. Earlier in his career, he was sent by the Spanish governor of Cuba to arrest Hernando Cortés as Cortés was conquering Montezuma's empire. Cortés defeated Narváez and his forces, and Narváez himself lost an eye in the battle. The historian Samuel Elliot Morrison described Narváez as both "cruel and stupid" and "the most incompetent of all who sailed for Spain in this era."

Nevertheless, the king of Spain later appointed Narváez governor general ("*adelantado*") of Florida, and Narváez set out to travel his dominion. His plan was to explore the largely unknown coastal area between what is now Soto la Marina in northeast Mexico and the Florida Keys, as well as, of course, to seek gold. Given the riches discovered by Cortés ten years earlier in Central Mexico, who knew what additional riches remained to be discovered in other areas of the Gulf?

Landing at Boca Ciega Bay

Narváez set sail from Cuba directly for northeast Mexico with five ships, four hundred men and women and eighty horses only to run into a hurricane. At this point, he changed course and sought safety in a Florida port, probably Tampa Bay. He could not find the entrance to Tampa Bay and ended up in Boca Ciega Bay instead. Upon reaching the bay, Narváez saw a cluster of huts on the shore, including one structure large enough to hold three hundred people, and sent a scouting party to investigate. This small party encountered a few friendly natives. The next day, Narváez himself went ashore only to find the area deserted. A search of the huts discovered a single gold object, a small rattle. But this was all that was needed to inspire Narváez to go on. After claiming the area for Spain, Narváez spent the next ten days exploring. The Spaniards found their way across a wide peninsula, eventually coming upon a large bay that Narváez christened La Bahia de las Cruz (the Bay of the Cross). However, Narváez still did not believe that this was Tampa Bay, and so he sent one of his ships north to find it.

Historian and archaeologist Jerald Milanich, at the Florida Museum of Natural History, believes that the reason Narváez did not think he was at Tampa Bay was that the Spanish were using maps with erroneous latitudes. Because of these errors, Narváez's pilot must have thought that he was near present-day Charlotte Harbor and that Tampa Bay was ninety miles to the north. The fact that Narváez's naval force found no harbor to the north of the original landing site strongly suggests that Narváez had, in fact, landed in the vicinity of Tampa Bay.

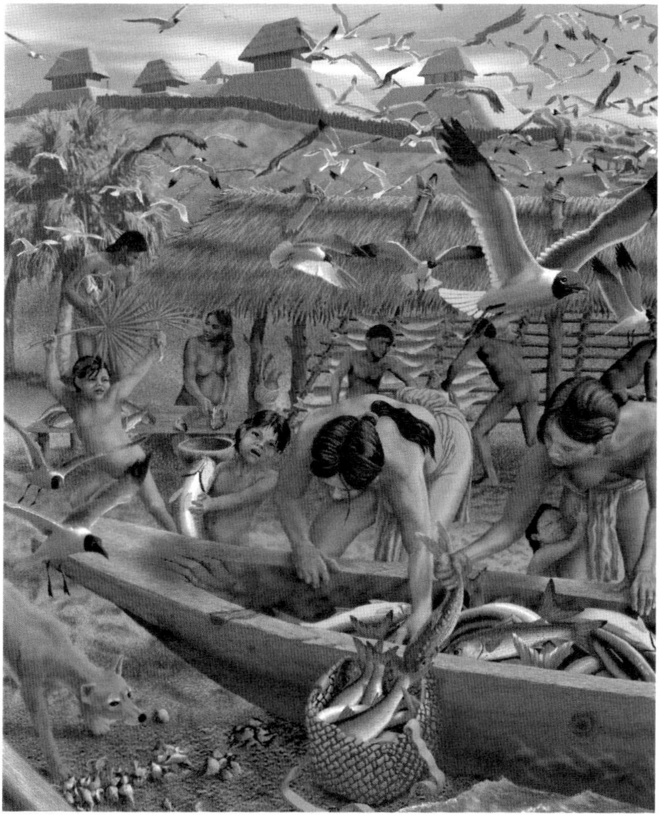

Left: Painting depicting Native American life in the Tampa Bay area at the time of the Spanish Entrada. *Courtesy Herman Trappman, artist.*

Below: Maximo Point near the mouth of Boca Ciega Bay in the early 1900s. Maximo Park, an important Indian mound site, is today part of St. Petersburg. These shores may have looked much the same in the sixteenth century when the Spanish arrived. Hugh C. Leighton Company postcard, postmarked 1910. *Courtesy Michaels Family Collection.*

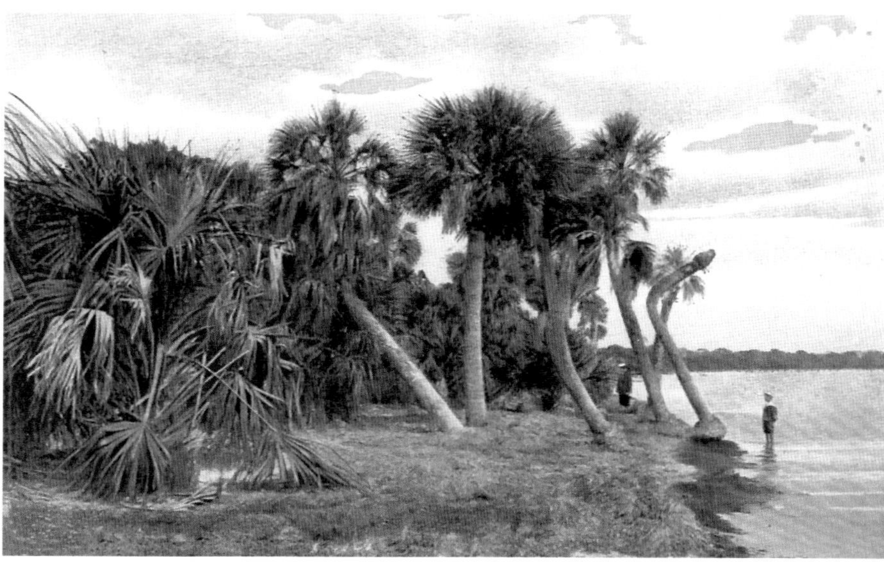

MELEE AT UCITA

At this point, Narváez encountered a small band of natives who directed him to a nearby village. Some earlier historians believed the village to be called Ucita and the village chief to be Hirrihigua. According to these historians, the chief took the Spaniards on a tour of the village. During the tour, they came upon a number of boxes made in Castile, Spain. Apparently, these had been retrieved by the natives from a Spanish shipwreck. To the Spaniards' astonishment, the boxes contained corpses wrapped in painted deerskins. Narváez burned the boxes and bodies, setting off a melee between the Spaniards and the natives. In the course of this battle, Hirrihigua's nose was cut off, and his mother was hacked to death and fed to Narváez's greyhounds.

The Spaniards then ransacked the village looking for gold and silver, and a few golden trinkets were discovered. Narváez demanded to know where he could find more. Perhaps as a ploy to get rid of the Spanish, the natives shouted out "Apalachen" and pointed to the north. At this point, Narváez made a fateful decision. He decided to split his forces, sending half on foot and horse by land through the Florida wilds to the north in search of Apalachen and sending his supply ships up the coast. The plan was to rendezvous at Tampa Bay, which he still believed to be to the north.

THE EXPEDITION'S TRAGIC END

For many weeks, Narváez's land forces wandered through the interior of Florida, finally reaching the heart of the Aplachee Indian country, near present-day Tallahassee, where they found not gold but a hostile people who attacked them. Meanwhile, Narváez's naval force gave up looking for him, and most of the ships returned to Cuba. Narváez eventually made his way to present-day St. Mark's Bay, where he built five small boats to carry the expedition's remaining 245 survivors to safety, or so he hoped. The remaining horses were killed and eaten, and their hides were used to make canteens for water. Of the 245 Spaniards who embarked on the five boats, only 81 made it safely as far as the Texas coast. This was six months after their arrival at Boca Ciega Bay. Eight years later, a mere 4 of these survived to reach a Spanish settlement in northern Mexico. One of these survivors was Álvar Núñez Cabeza de Vaca, the treasurer of the expedition. De Vaca wrote a memoir of the adventure that is fascinating reading.

Princess Hirrihigua and Pocahontas

The Narváez story has a sequel. Narváez's wife organized a rescue expedition. On this expedition was a young sailor named Juan Ortiz. The expedition returned to Tampa Bay, hoping that perhaps Narváez had come back to his original point of departure, or at least to find some clue of his whereabouts. While sailing in the bay, the expedition saw some natives place a piece of paper on a cane and set it in the sand. Ortiz and a few companions left the ship by dinghy to retrieve the paper. As soon as they reached the shore, the natives set upon them. Ortiz's companions were soon killed. Ortiz himself was taken captive by Hirrihigua, chief of the village of Ucita. He soon found himself being roasted alive over an open fire. As his screams went out, Hirrihigua's wife or daughter (depending on which account you read) interceded on his behalf and persuaded her husband to stop the roast. Later, his oldest daughter arranged Ortiz's escape to the nearby village of Mocoso. Hirrihigua's daughter was betrothed to the chief of Mocoso. But the Mocoso chief's protection of Ortiz cost him his planned marriage to Hirrihigua's daughter.

It is reported that Captain John Smith of Jamestown later read about Ortiz's story and was inspired to claim a similar event by another Indian maiden whom we all know as Pocahontas. The first account of the Juan Ortiz story appeared in print in 1557, long before Captain Smith left for Jamestown in 1606. Ortiz was later rescued by Hernando de Soto in 1539. He served as an invaluable interpreter for the De Soto expedition.

Instant History Replay

This account of Narváez's activities on the Pinellas Peninsula can be found in local histories, commemorative plaques and museum exhibits. However, a careful rereading of the original Spanish accounts of the Narváez expedition and recent archaeological evidence cast doubt on some of the more celebrated events.

There are two eyewitness accounts of the Narváez landing and expedition. Both of these were written by Cabeza de Vaca, one with input from the other three expedition survivors. None of these accounts mention a village called Ucita or a chief named Hirrihigua. Instead, current historians and archaeologists such as Milanich believe that the village discovered by Narváez was Tocobaga, located at what we now call Safety Harbor. This seems to fit with the De Vaca account that stated that Narváez left his base camp, penetrated inland and followed the shore of the bay to the village at the head of the bay. It has also been established through archaeological evidence that an Ucita village existed not on the Pinellas Peninsula but rather on the other side of Tampa Bay, at the mouth of the Little Manatee River. Further, there is no mention of a melee between the local natives and the Narváez expedition in De Vaca's account, an event unlikely to be omitted.

There are four accounts of the De Soto expedition that rescued Juan Ortiz. Eyewitnesses to the De Soto expedition wrote three of these. None of these eyewitnesses refer to the chief of Ucita as Hirrihigua, but instead they give the name of the chief as the same name as the village, Ucita. In fact, De Vaca stated in his chronicle that the expedition did not encounter a chief whose name was different from the province or village he ruled until after moving north of the Tampa Bay area. Archaeologist B.W. Burger noted that names mentioned may reflect actual chiefs, temporary headmen, villages, geographic areas, dialectical subgroups, larger language stocks or combinations of these.

THE INCA

So where did the legend of Narváez's melee with Hirrihigua at the village of Ucita come from? The answer is "The Inca," also referred to as the "Gentleman of Elvas" and more formally known as Garcilaso de la Vega. De la Vega was the son of a Spanish conquistador and an Inca princess, and known as The Inca. He was not an eyewitness to the Narváez expedition or even the De Soto expedition. He completed his account of the De Soto expedition (with references to the Narváez expedition) in 1591, fifty-two years after the De Soto expedition and sixty-three years after the Narváez expedition. Folklorist George Lankford wrote that The Inca "probably used

Elvas [one of the De Soto expedition eyewitnesses], the written sources The Inca claimed to have used, and oral testimony in the form of folkloric legends gathered from Gonzalo Silvestre [a De Soto expedition survivor]. All were woven into a text fitting certain literary canons of the time. The result has been an enjoyable tale read ever since and used by most popular writers as their basis for retelling the De Soto story"—and, one might add, the Narváez story as well.

TAMPA BAY AT LAST

Narváez was seeking Tampa Bay. Somehow, he missed the entrance and ended up in adjacent Boca Ciega Bay. He split his foot and horse soldiers from his naval supply ships. The ships sought to rendezvous with him to the north. Upon their return south, they finally discovered Tampa Bay. As de Vaca reported in his chronicle, "[F]ive leagues below the place where we had disembarked they found the port that extended seven or eight leagues into the land and which was the same one we had discovered when we found the cases from Castile…containing the dead bodies, which were of Christian men." Here we likely have a clash of cultures. Narváez perhaps burned them as the most expeditious way to prevent violation of their remains. On the other hand, perhaps the natives intended to honor the dead by keeping them in the Castilian boxes. The discovery of the dead Spaniards may not have been the provocation leading to a melee.

De Vaca went on to declare Tampa's port "the best in the world, extending seven or eight leagues into the land, and at the entrance it has six fathoms of water and five along the shoreline, the bottom is smooth, no sea breaks upon it, nor any boisterous storms. It can contain many vessels and the fish are plentiful."

EPILOGUE

In 1966, a local science teacher and amateur archaeologist by the name of Frank Bushnell claimed to have located Narváez's campsite on the east side of Boca Ciega Bay near what is now the 1600 block of Park Street North. This

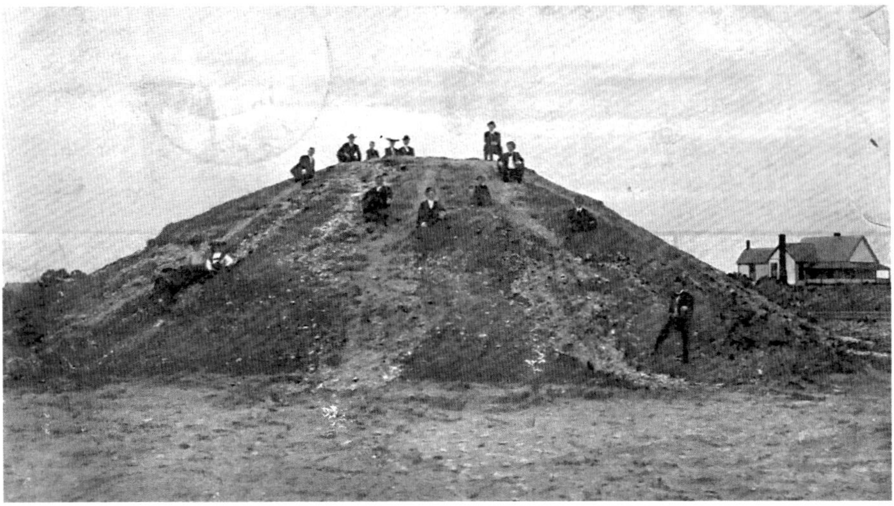

Indian mounds such as this abounded throughout the St. Petersburg waterfront at the turn of the last century. Raphael Tuck & Sons, postmarked 1908. *Michaels Family Collection.*

site is now known as the Anderson Site, named after the owners. In 1998 a second excavation of the Anderson Site was completed by the Central Gulf Coast Archaeological Society. This excavation found extensive evidence of native occupation and some evidence of Spanish contact. However, there was nothing found to firmly document Spanish contact dating as early as the Narváez landing. Oral histories included with the society's findings also noted report of a Spanish sword found years earlier. However, the sword itself has long since disappeared.

No gold was found.

NOTE ON THE IMPACT OF THE NARVÁEZ ENTRADA

Narváez's expedition was the first major expedition to explore the interior of Florida and the Gulf Coast states. Other expeditions were limited to coastal areas, with limited penetration of the interior. The impact of the Narváez expedition on the Indian population may have been immense. Some authorities mention a possible impact in terms of the spread of illness to Native Americans lacking immunity, as well as military contact. The greater impact may have been cultural. Cabeza de Vaca and the other final survivors were treated as quasi-deities by native peoples in the Gulf Coast states. Cabeza de Vaca's written account of his ordeal itself had a major impact. The account significantly inspired further attempts at exploration and European settlement. The account is known to have directly inspired a Franciscan priest, Father Marcos de Nica, to lead a small expedition northward from Mexico in 1539. One of his companions was a survivor of the Narváez expedition. That expedition, in turn, led to Francisco de Vasquez de Coronado's 1642 expedition into the southwest United States. Hernando de Soto's 1539 expedition, also launched from the Tampa Bay area, was greatly influenced by Narváez's earlier *entrada*. While the term *entrada* refers to the first expedition and conquest of a territory, the word literally means "entrance." The St. Petersburg and Tampa Bay area served literally as the "entrance" to two of the most significant Spanish explorations of the New World.

Sources used in this chapter include Raymond Arsenault, *St. Petersburg and the Florida Dream 1888–1950*; B.W. Burger, "The People in Between: Tampa Bay Natives From Contact to Extinction"; Charles C. Mann, *1491: New Revelations of the Americans Before Columbus*; Bernal Diaz Castillo, *The Discovery and Conquest of Mexico*; Rodgrigo Ranjel, "A Narrative of DeSoto's Expedition," in *Narratives of the Career of Hernando de Soto in the Conquest of Florida*, edited by Edward G. Bourne; Walter P. Fuller, *St. Petersburg and Its People*; Garcilaso de la Vega, *History of the Conquest of Florida*, translated by Charmion Shelby; John H. Hann, *Indians of Central and South Florida, 1513–1763*; Will Michaels, "The Spanish Invasion at Boca Ciega Bay," *South Beaches Journal*, 2007; Jerald T. Milanich, *Florida Indians and the Invasion from Europe*; Lawrence A. Clayton, Vernon James Knight Jr. and Edwards C. Moore, eds., *The De Soto Chronicles: The Expedition of Hernando De Soto to North America 1539–1543*; Paul Schneider, *Brutal Journey: The Epic Story of the First Crossing of North America*; John R. Swanton, *Final Report of the United States De Soto Expedition Commission*; Terrance L. Simpson, *The Narvaez/Anderson Site (8Pi54): A Safety Harbor Culture Shell Mound and Midden—AD 1000–1600*; and communication with Jeff Moates.

The Great Hurricanes

While there have been many near-miss hurricanes in the Tampa Bay area, there are only two so far that have really made the history books: the hurricanes of 1848 and 1921.

On September 23, 1848, a hundred-year storm hit Tampa Bay. After two days of gales and atmospheric turbulence, hurricane-force winds roared into Tampa Bay. While the storm's peak winds were reported to be relatively low for hurricanes at ninety to one hundred miles per hour, and barometric pressure of 29.18 inches did not equal those of many other storms, the tidal surge was the highest ever recorded. This was because of the direction and pace of the storm. The storm hugged the coastline as it moved north from the Florida Keys. As the eye of the storm approached the Pinellas Peninsula, the normally lake-like waters of the Gulf were pushed into Tampa Bay. Once the eye had passed, the wind direction suddenly reversed, and within a few hours' time, a wall of water nearly fifteen feet high raced from Egmont Key to the head of Tampa Bay and back again. At one point, large sections of the peninsula were under water, the waves reaching the treetops in low-lying areas.

Results were devastating. All of the buildings at Fort Brooke in Tampa were badly damaged, and much of Tampa washed away. Ships were tossed about like toys. A schooner came to rest several hundred yards inland on the Tampa side. Piers and wharves were destroyed. The lighthouse at Egmont Key had just been built. At the time, it was the only lighthouse between St. Marks and Key West. When the lighthouse keeper at Egmont Key, Marvel

Edwards, saw that the tide was going to overflow the island, he placed his family in his boat and waded with it to the middle of the island. There he secured the boat to a tree. Tides 15 feet above normal washed over the island. Edwards's boat was lifted almost to the top of the tree. The 120-foot lighthouse that had just been built had its foundation undercut by the water, and the tower cracked and leaned like the Tower of Pisa. While Edwards and his family survived, he was so traumatized by the catastrophe that he resigned his post.

Early pioneers John Levick and Joe Silva were sailing on their way back from New Orleans when the storm hit. Upon their return, they found the Pinellas coastline completely changed. They sailed into Boca Ciega Bay through a 180-foot-wide channel that had not been there when they left. The channel was later named John's Pass after John Levick.

Other early pioneers were also affected. Antonio Maximo Hernandez, after whom Maximo Point is named, had his fish rancho at Frenchman's Creek completely destroyed. He left for Havana and never returned. Odet Philippe survived the storm by scrambling up an Indian mound near his St. Helena plantation in what is now Safety Harbor. The mound was partly washed away.

While the early pioneers were shaken by the storm, the long-term impact was on the environment. After the storm passed, much of the local landscape was radically changed. Islands were sliced in two. What was once high ground became marshland. New channels and inlets appeared. The barrier islands were completely changed. Palm Island was sliced in half, becoming Pine and Cabbage Keys. The Isle of Palms and the Isle of Capri were separated from Treasure Island. Plants and animals were forced to adapt to new surroundings. Whole forests were uprooted or destroyed by saltwater contamination.

THE GREAT HURRICANE OF 1921

On October 25, 1921, seventy-three years after the hurricane of 1848, another hurricane hit Tampa Bay by way of Tarpon Springs. Known as the Tarpon Springs Hurricane, this storm at one point reached Category 4 status, with winds of 140 miles per hour while out over the Gulf. But by the time it came ashore near Tarpon Springs, wind gusts had fallen to 100 miles per hour. A six- to eleven-foot storm surge flooded low-lying areas. All across Pinellas County, windows were broken and power and telephone lines were down. But the greatest damage occurred along the waterfront, where boats were smashed and the St. Petersburg Municipal Pier was badly damaged. Other boats in the bay were sunk outright. On the Gulf side, the Pass-a-Grille and Seminole Bridges were completely destroyed. There was a rumor that scores were drowned at Pass-a-Grille; fortunately, this turned out to be false. Loss of life was limited to two persons in St. Petersburg and perhaps another six in other areas of the county.

While major changes in the landscape were not nearly as significant as in the 1848 storm, Caladesi Island was formed from Honeymoon Island in the Dunedin area. The new channel between the islands was aptly called Hurricane Pass. However, Myrtle Scharrer Betz, who weathered the hurricane on Caladesi Island, reported in her memoirs no damage to her father's homestead there. It is estimated that about $3 million in damage was done (1921 dollars). George S. (Gidge) Gandy Jr., son of George S. Gandy Sr. (who built the Gandy Bridge), reported in a 1957 newspaper article that tidal water was much lower at Pass-a-Grille than at St. Petersburg. It was highest at the top of Tampa Bay in the vicinity of Oldsmar, where water reached fourteen feet above normal.

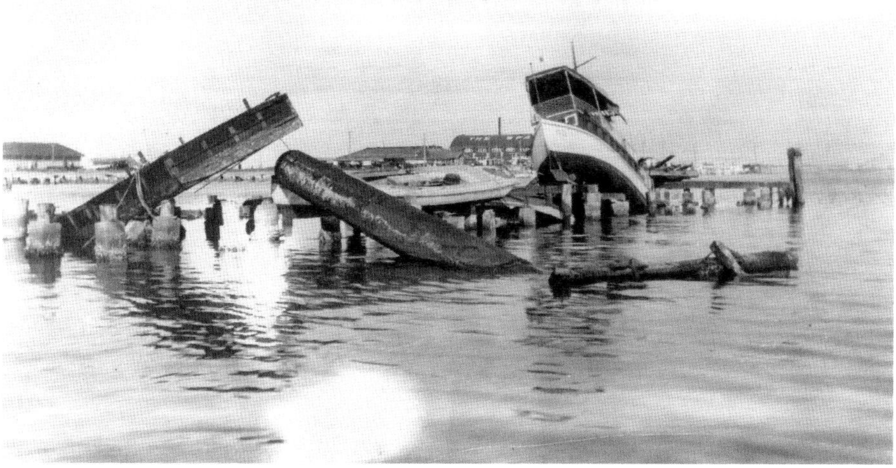

Waterfront damage from the 1921 hurricane in the Central Yacht Basin. The Spa is left of the elevated boat. Mayor Noel Mitchell was energetic in repairing the hurricane damage and restoring the city to normality, image 1921. *Courtesy St. Petersburg Museum of History.*

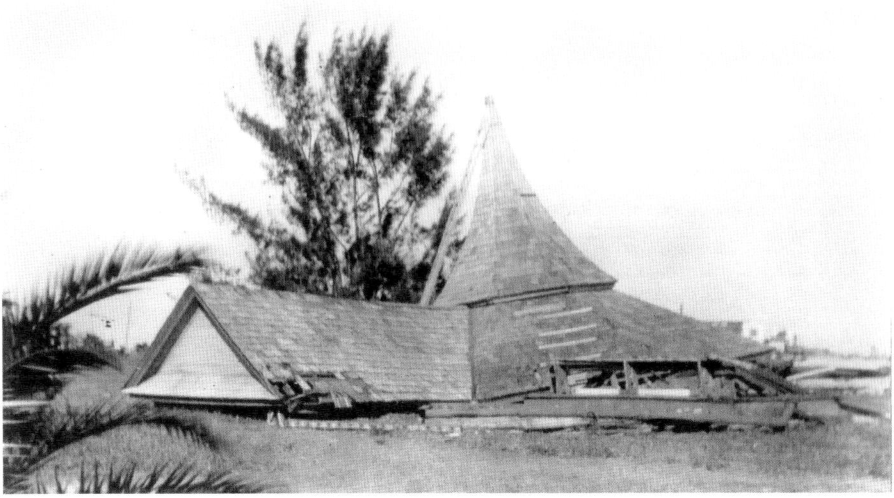

Bandstand at Waterfront Park shortly after the 1921 hurricane, image 1921. *Courtesy St. Petersburg Museum of History.*

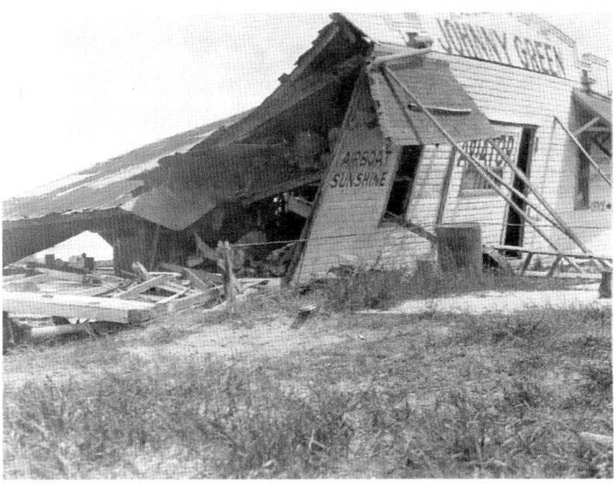

It does not take a direct hit for a hurricane to do severe damage. This 1926 photo shows early St. Petersburg pilot Johnny Green's hangar on the site of today's Vinoy Hotel after it was damaged by the 1926 hurricane that crossed the state from the east coast. At the time, Green flew the Curtiss Flying Boat *Sunshine*. Green held an early flight record for altitude, image 1926. *Courtesy Michaels Family Collection.*

While no lives were lost at Pass-a-Grille, the island was flooded. People rowed boats up Eighth Avenue. The boardwalk was destroyed. The casino extending into the Gulf at the foot of Twenty-third Avenue was demolished, and the Pass-a-Grille Hotel was severely damaged. The St. Petersburg Beach Hotel and Casino operated by George Lizotte on Blind Pass at about Seventy-fifth Avenue was washed away. Lizotte described the scene:

> *Dining room tables were floating around and we had to swim to the staircase. We had been there but a short time when the south veranda was*

> *torn away and carried over the top of the casino…we silently watched huge waves demolishing the hotel whose roof was lifted bodily and blown away. Furniture piled up in heaps against front rooms, acted as battering rams against the wall, which gradually gave way, and the whole mass floated away, leaving only the foundation as a reminder that a 50-room hotel had been in operation there.*

While parts of Pass-a-Grille were hard hit, little damage of note occurred farther north at Indian Rocks Beach.

There are few people living who still remember the 1921 hurricane. Helen Gandy O'Brien, daughter of Gidge Gandy, remembered that her father later told her how worried he was about their new home, known as Mullet Farm, in what is now the Driftwood neighborhood of St. Petersburg. The home was surrounded by water, but none entered the house. Gidge drove a nail on a post supporting the house to mark the water level. However, many other homes were flooded as far as five blocks in from Big Bayou.

Jim Franklin Sirmons was just three years old at the time of the 1921 hurricane. The fact that he had distinct recollections of this event speaks to the trauma he experienced. At the time of the storm, he lived just south of Booker Creek in St. Petersburg with his parents, B.F. and Pearl Sirmons, and his brother. He remembered the storm as "ferocious…I could feel the house moving off its foundations. My mother barricaded us in an inner bedroom and we hid under the double bed. Trees could be heard banging on the house. There was total desolation. Our small barn was blown away. The animals were totally disoriented. There were lots of snakes about that I had never seen before. I remember how frightened and scared my mother was. God, it was frightening." Jim continued to live and grow up in St. Petersburg. He graduated from the University of Florida in 1939 and later became vice-president of CBS, with responsibility for radio and later for TV production.

Fisherman "Florida" George Roberts lost everything during the great hurricane of 1921: fish house, several boats, nets and all his fishing gear and tools. After the hurricane, Florida got a job with the government salvaging boats that had been sunk. He earned enough to rebuild his party boat business and even used some of the salvage to build himself a new boat named *Ain't We Got Fun*, known as simply *Fun* for short. One of his other boats was called the *Leak-a-Lot*!

But it did not take a hurricane to cause misery to our early settlers. In October 1924, Florida George, his wife, Elda May, and their three children were living in a palmetto shack in today's Fort De Soto area when they experienced a tropical storm. Not having the advantage of TV or even radio, Florida had to use his weather smarts to anticipate the coming storm. His preparations included fastening two steel cables over the roof of the palmetto shack. He moved the *Fun* to the protected side of the key. "We could hear the mangrove and buttonwood trees snapping as they crashed to the ground." The water rose to eighteen inches on the floor of the shack. Florida brought a plank into the shack to put across the rafters for the family to sit on should the water rise higher. Fortunately, it did not. "Nice to have a sand floor. So easy to clean up after such an ordeal."

In 1926, St. Petersburg was severely affected by a hurricane that first hit the east coast of Florida and then crossed the state. This time, the Robertses were living in the old Will and Silas Dent house on Cabbage Key. Florida reassured his family, "I don't believe this one will be too bad and we are ready for it anyway. Be a lot more comfortable here than crowded in with some scared folks in St. Petersburg." It turned out there were some scared folks on Cabbage Key. The ground flooded, carrying huge logs and all sorts of debris toward the bay. Heavy objects struck the concrete pillars of the house foundation. "The tide had risen so rapidly that the house was set in the middle of a raging river." Part of the roof blew off, and the window at the head of the stairs blew in. Miraculously, the Roberts family rode out the storm unhurt.

While many persons, especially fishermen such as George Roberts, lost all they had in the 1921 hurricane, the storm was downplayed by local government and business interests. They were concerned that the tourist trade might be harmed. Damage was rapidly cleared. The Pass-a-Grille Bridge was quickly rebuilt, and the St. Petersburg Municipal Pier was repaired and reopened two months after the hurricane hit.

History is instructive. Upon reaching Tampa Bay, both the 1848 and 1921 storms were what we now classify as Category 1 and 2 hurricanes. Yet, partly because of the particular manner in which they approached Tampa Bay, they created immense destruction. Only a handful of early pioneers lived in all of Pinellas County in 1848. In 1921, Pinellas County's largest city, St. Petersburg, had about 14,000 permanent residents. Now there are 255,000 permanent residents living in St. Petersburg and 918,000 in Pinellas County as a whole. Development has also increased exponentially. Despite the fact that many structures are now built much stronger and extensive attention has been given to emergency planning, a recurrence of hurricanes similar to those of 1848 or 1921 today could still bring serious disaster.

Sources used in this chapter include Raymond Arsenault, *St. Petersburg and the Florida Dream*; John A. Bethell, *History of Pinellas Point*; Myrtle Scharrer Betz, *Yesteryear I Lived in Paradise: The Story of Caladesi Island*; Frank T. Hurley Jr., *Surf, Sand & Post Card Sunsets*; Will Michaels, "The Great Hurricanes of 1848 and 1921," *Northeast Journal*, 2007; Elda M. Roberts, *The Stubborn Fisherman*; the *St. Petersburg Times*; and interviews with Helen Gandy O'Brien and Jim Sirmons.

Civil War in St. Pete

In November 1860, Abraham Lincoln was elected president, but not with any votes from Florida. In fact, he was not even on the Florida ballot. Florida seceded from the Union on January 10, 1861. While the state of Florida seceded in 1861, Hillsborough County (which at the time included Pinellas) actually seceded on November 24, 1860, with 106 prominent citizens signing a declaration of secession. About 16,000 Floridians fought in the Civil War, and 5,000 of these died, out of an 1860 population of 140,424 (some 62,000 of these estimated to be African Americans, mostly slaves). Fort Brooke in Tampa was a Confederate strongpoint until its surrender in April 1864. Tallahassee was the only Southern capital east of the Mississippi to be spared destruction by the Union, due to a spirited defense put up by the local militia and cadets from West Florida Seminary (today's Florida State University). On April 1, 1865, Florida governor John Milton committed suicide with a shotgun rather than accept loss of the war.

The first Southern Civil War unit to operate in Pinellas was a volunteer company formed in the upper county area on July 20, 1861. It had an enrollment of 60 persons out of a county population of 381. The company only operated for about three months. A small Coastal Guard unit was formed in July 1861 and operated for only a few months. Eventually, Company K, Seventh Florida Infantry Regiment, was formed in April 1862 and operated until the end of the war.

John A. Bethell was an early settler who lived in what is today the Driftwood neighborhood of St. Petersburg on Big Bayou. He was a member

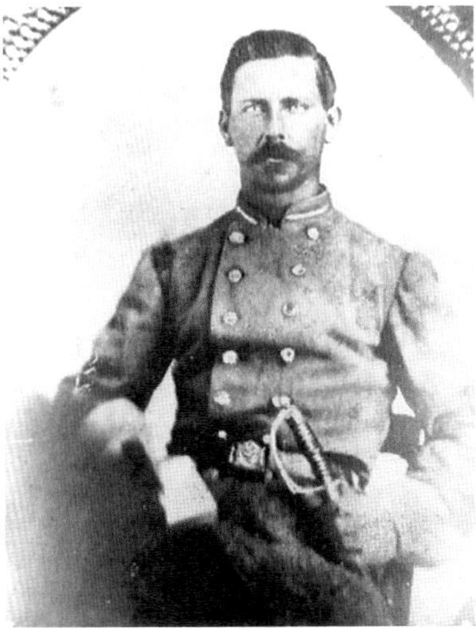

An 1862 image of Confederate lieutenant John A. Bethell of Company K, Florida Seventh Infantry Regiment. Before enlisting in Company K, Bethell was a member of the Florida Volunteer Coast Guard Company. He was a friend of Abel Miranda and witnessed the raid on Miranda's homestead. Bethell is buried at the Greenwood Cemetery in south St. Petersburg. *Courtesy St. Petersburg Museum of History.*

of the Florida Volunteer Coast Guard Company with Robert Watson and later became a Confederate lieutenant with Company K. Watson was originally a resident of Key West, which remained in Union control throughout the war. Watson left Key West and went to Tampa Bay at the outset of the war to fight for the Confederacy. By profession he was a carpenter. Beginning on January 1, 1862, Watson recorded in his diary that he was at "Point Pinellas Station, Ft. Buckley." Whether he was being facetious about "Ft. Buckley" is unclear. We are aware of no other reference to such a name, but there was a soldier by the name of Buckley in his company who he may have decided to "honor." However, the Confederate base camp in Pinellas is known to have been somewhere around Big Bayou, perhaps at today's Coquina Key.

Shortly thereafter, the company was designated the "Key West Avengers," several of the company, including Watson, having come from Key West. The company elected its own officers and had at its disposal several ships, including the *Kate Dale* (later renamed the *Josephine*), the *Mollie Post* and the *Mary Jane*. Later, they were broken up into two guerrilla companies, each with thirty-four "rank and file" men. In April 1862, they became Company K. John Bethell was elected third lieutenant. Robert Watson was designated second sergeant. Watson was promoted to full first sergeant in August 1862.

In June 1862, Company K left Florida to support the Confederate army in Tennessee and Kentucky. While there, Watson became sick and was captured by the Yankees along with several others. Because of their illness, the Yankees paroled them. In order to deal with large numbers of captured troops early in the Civil War, the U.S. and Confederate governments relied on the traditional European system of parole and exchange of prisoners. The terms called for prisoners to give their word not to take up arms against their captors until they were formally exchanged for an enemy captive of equal rank. As a parolee, Watson made his way back to Tampa, where he eventually received notice of his exchange. He then returned to his company and combat.

Beginning in the fall of 1861, a small fleet of Union blockaders was stationed at Egmont Key (later known as Fort Dade), an island at the entrance to Tampa Bay. During the Third Seminole War in 1849, none other than Colonel Robert E. Lee surveyed the Gulf Coast and recommended that Egmont Key be set aside as a federal military reservation. According to local historian Ray Arsenault, the Pinellas Peninsula played an indirect role in the Union's campaign to blockade Florida's Gulf Coast. The Gulf Coast was an important source of salt and beef for the Confederate army. Salt was so important that salt workers were one of two occupations exempt from Confederate conscription (the other being clergy). A number of salt evaporation operations were located on Tampa Bay, and these were prime targets for the Union navy. One successful attack was made at Rocky Point (now the east end of the Courtney Campbell Causeway) in December 1864, destroying seven large boilers. Another major saltworks was destroyed at Alligator Creek near Safety Harbor.

For a time, Unionists tried to live on the mainland, but sooner or later they were killed or driven out by the local Confederate Home Guard. Egmont Key also served as a refuge for a minority of local residents who were pro-Union. How big a minority is unclear, but in April 1862, one Union flag officer reported "a strong Union feeling in west Florida, kept under only by want of arms and means of resistance to the secession party." Historian Karl Grismer reported that "it is a fact that there was a sharp division among the pioneer settlers during the war. Some of the pioneers were strong northern sympathizers and when the 'rebels' turned on them they sought refuge at Egmont Key."

According to John E. Whitehurst, who resided some eight to ten miles from "Old Tampa" on the shores of the bay (present-day Safety Harbor), some thirty-eight of his neighbors and friends living within six miles of him were Unionists. Whitehurst sought the protection of the Union navy at Egmont Key and provided them considerable intelligence. His nephew, Winfied Scott Whitehurst, also sought protection. At one point, there were as many as twenty-five Unionists and their families given protection at Egmont. A greater number than that actually passed through Egmont as they were evacuated to the North. One of these was James Hay, who lived in the Clam Bayou area (near present-day Twin Brooks Golf Course). Hay was one of only five families living in the South Pinellas Peninsula at the time. None of the Egmont refugees is known to have ever returned to the peninsula. The Unionists were referred to by Robert Watson as "Tories" or "Lincolnites." Additionally, according to historian Walter P. Fuller, there were sixty slaves in mid-Pinellas in 1860.

Some of the Union naval ships that participated in the blockade included the *Ethan Allen*, *Tahoma*, *Sunflower*, *Pursuit* and *Beauregard*. Confederate blockade runners captured or destroyed by the Union forces included the *Salvor*, *Scottish Chief* (owned by James McKay, father of a Tampa mayor and newspaper publisher), *Silas Henry*, *Mary Nevis*, *Teresa* (flying British colors for purposes of deception, something the Confederates also reported being done by the Federals), *Annie B.*, *Olive Branch* and *Crazy Jane*. These ships usually carried cotton, turpentine, rosin and pine tar extracted from Florida pine trees and used for caulking and waterproofing ships and as a solvent.

Union officers reported that the blockade was a great success and that West Florida was in great distress. The economic impact was reflected in the high cost of foodstuffs—coffee at $1.00 and tea at $2.00 per pound and a barrel of pork at $60.00. In January 1863, Robert Watson wrote while in Tampa that

> [t]*imes are very hard in this place now. Corn meal is selling for $5.00 per bushel, sweet potatoes $1.50 per bushel and seldom to be had at that price. Not a pound of beef in the market for the cattle owners will not sell their cattle to the butcher for any price for Confederate money and there is no gold or silver to be had in the country. Fresh pork, when to be had, which is seldom, sells readily for 20 cents a pound head, Hoofs and all. Once in a while a little rice is brought in from the country and sells for 15 cents a pound, salt $10.00 per bushel, sugar* [omission] *cents per Lb., molasses $1.50 per gal. and everything else in proportion.*

On the other hand, he reported successfully hunting for deer and "millions of all kinds" of fish in Coffee Pot Bayou, "and they bite well."

Life for the soldier and sailor at Point Pinellas and Tampa Bay had both its good times and bad. When winds were calm on the bay, ships would need to be pulled by rowing for long distances. On one occasion, Robert Watson wrote, "After breakfast I went into the woods and cut a mast for our boats… Ended the evening by singing songs, telling stories, etc. The fleas were so savage I could not sleep." He was not always pleased to have company either. His boat company once rendezvoused with a Confederate horse company.

"The horse company are all growling and dissatisfied, they don't want to stand guard. I hope they will go away soon for they are the laziest, dirtiest and lousiest set of men that I ever saw."

The Confederate force in Pinellas was not limited to Southern whites. Watson wrote in his diary, "Truly this is a cosmopolitan company, it is composed of Yankees, Crackers, Conchs, Englishmen, Spaniards, Germans, Frenchmen, Italians, Poles, Irishmen, Swedes, Chinese, Portuguese, Brazilians, 1 Rock Scorpio Crusoe [referring to Mr. Crusoe, a native of Gibraltar, where the locals are referred to as "Rock Scorpions"]; some half Indians, surely this is the greatest mixture of nations for a small country I have ever heard of." According to notes left by Watson descendant Caroline Condrick, there was also a black man.

Military engagements on land in the Tampa Bay area were occasional. One of these occurred on March 27, 1863, at Gadsden Point (southern tip of what is now MacDill Air Force Base). Three persons signaled the Union ship *Pursuit* from the shore by building a small fire and waving a flag of truce. Two were dressed in female attire, with their hands and faces blackened. One of them was reported to have been "overcome with joy," exclaiming, "Thank God, thank God, I am free." The Union ship sent a cutter to investigate under a flag of truce, only to encounter one hundred armed rebels rising from the bushes. The rebels ignored the Union white flag and opened fire. In the exchange that followed, four Union sailors were shot, one suffering a fractured humerus and a second who was shot in the "right upper lip, the ball striking the teeth, came out below, and extended to the jaw." Somehow they survived and were rescued by their mother ship. A number of rebels were also hit by Union fire.

On October 16, 1863, the Union sent shore parties in pursuit of the Confederate blockade runners *Scottish Chief* and *Kate Dale* (later renamed the *Josephine*). The Confederates tried to protect the ships by anchoring them in the Hillsborough River. The Union force was successful in destroying the *Scottish Chief* and damaging the *Kate Dale*. These ships were loaded with cotton. Some of the rebel crew were captured. An anchor and davit from the *Scottish Chief* are on display at Veteran's Park in Tampa. Tampa was bombarded by Union Forces six times, twice in 1862, three times in 1863 and again in 1864.

After serving in the Tampa Bay area, Watson was sent north to Tennessee. Loyal Confederate that he was, Watson was not pleased with his treatment by the Confederate army outside of Tampa Bay:

> *Confederate soldiers are treated like dogs everywhere that I have been since I left Tampa. They are not allowed on half the rations that the army regulations call for*[,] *for the quartermasters and other officers give them just what they like and pocket the balance and yet the soldiers knowing all this are foolish enough to put up with it. They grumble and growl among themselves but never try to get redress for their wrongs. Men are kept in the hospitals when the doctors know that they will never recover while in the hospital, yet they will not give them furloughs to go home but keep them here to die. 7 and 8 is the average of deaths per day here.*

The most noted Civil War event to occur in South Pinellas was the 1862 Union naval raid that resulted in the burning and looting of the Abel Miranda homestead at Big Bayou. Abel Miranda had come to Pinellas with his wife, Eliza, from St. Augustine in 1857. According to John Bethell, writing many years later, this occurred in February. Robert Watson reported in his diary receiving information about this raid on March 16, suggesting a somewhat later date. Historian Fuller used this date for the raid. No Union report on the raid has been found.

Here is some of Bethell's account:

> *The* [Union] *smack was furnished with cannon and plenty of ammunition, including shot and shell. This outfit anchored off the Bayou some time before sunrise. About 7 a.m. they opened fire with round shot. They made three good line shots for the house…That was the first time we ever heard cannon shot whistle over our heads, but we knew there was no danger so long as they were up in the air. They then quit until about 8 a.m., when they again opened, with shell this time. I do not remember just how many were fired in all, but the first burst, as we thought, about ten feet over our heads, as we were standing out in front of the porch. It seemed like the heavens had fallen through, and scared us so that we did not know whether we were killed or just paralyzed.*

John Bethell and the Miranda family then fled the homestead. When Bethell returned, he found the house and outbuildings burned and chickens and shoats (young hogs) maimed. Even an old saddle was slashed. A great deal of other livestock and foodstuffs had been taken away by the Union, along with four boats. One of those participating in the attack was a boat captain from Key West who was a friend of Miranda's. Whether his participation was under duress or not is unknown. After the war, the captain

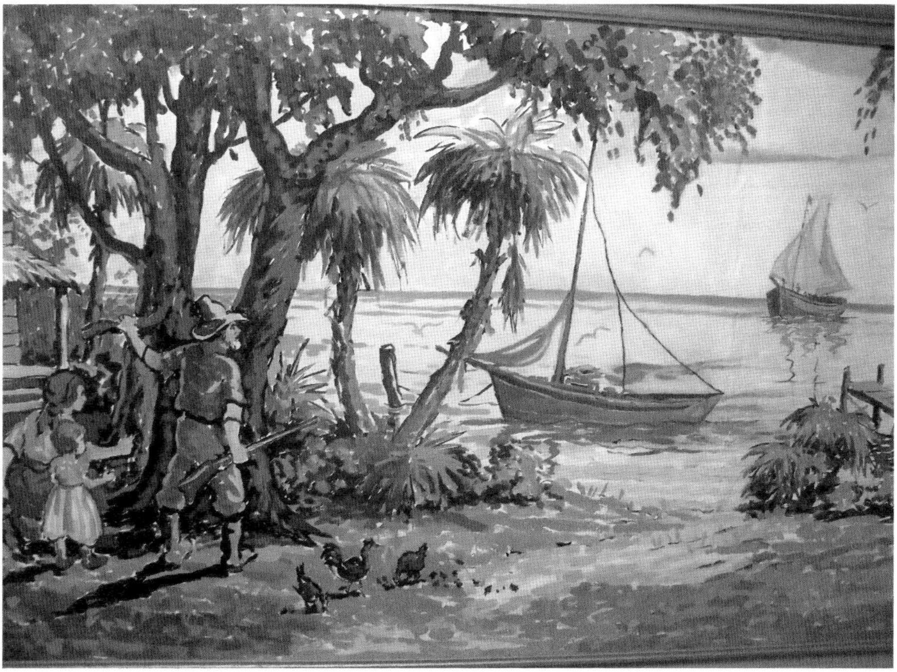

Painting by Mark Dixon Dodd depicting the Union raid on Abel Miranda's homestead in 1862. Dodd designed homes in the Driftwood neighborhood, where Miranda's home was located. He painted pictures depicting the history of the neighborhood as a way to interest buyers. Several of Dodd's paintings, including this one, may be found at the St. Petersburg Museum of History. *Courtesy Michaels Family Collection.*

sent Miranda a letter offering regret for his part in the raid and containing some jewelry that belonged to Eliza Miranda. Many years later, a resident of the Driftwood neighborhood near Big Bayou turned up an unexploded six-inch shell. He showed it to John Bethell, who exclaimed, "Why that's the shell that didn't explode! I always wondered what happened to it." The shell is now on display at the St. Petersburg Museum of History.

The motivation for this raid is murky. Some said that Miranda killed a Unionist by the name of Scott Whitehurst and that the raid was conducted in retaliation. However, official U.S. Navy records indicate that Whitehurst was actually killed after the raid. On September 3, 1862, the lieutenant commanding the U.S. gunboat *Tahoma* wrote:

> *I have the honor to report that on the 26th August…while three of the refugees who have been for some months at the lighthouse on Egmont Key*

> *under the protection of the United States were on the mainland endeavoring to procure potatoes, beef, etc., from their own farms near Old Tampa* [Safety Harbor] *for the support of themselves and their families, two of them, John and Scott Whitehurst, while shoving from the shore in their boat were barbarously set upon by guerrillas, and Scott Whitehurst was immediately killed and John Whitehurst mortally wounded...the third man, named Arnold, is supposed to have been murdered the same day...All these men were Union men.*

He went on to note that John Whitehurst asked that his three little sons be received into the United States naval service: "These guerrillas are scouring the woods, looking after deserters and conscripts; they rob, murder, and steal indiscriminately, if the reports of the refugees are to be credited; Union men they threaten to hang, and do shoot, as we have lamentable proof. It is said that every man capable of bearing arms has been forced to join the rebels in this part of Florida." Corinna Lowe Condrick, in her annotations to her relative Robert Watson's diary, noted that "Maranda [Miranda] raiders killed the Whitehursts when they came home (to Largo) Indian Rocks to get honey and red meat—young cattle."

It may be that the Unionists were simply looking to inflict damage to the property of a known local blockade runner and to secure badly needed supplies for the troops and Union supporters living at Egmont Key. Also, the Confederate base camp ("Pinellas Point Station") appears to have been located in the vicinity of Big Bayou. The Union forces may have assumed that Miranda was actively supporting the Confederates. Exactly how active Miranda was in the Confederate cause before the raid is unknown. Walter Fuller said beyond question that he was deeply involved in blockade running. According to John Bethell's daughters, Miranda was not active until after the attack, and he is not mentioned by Watson as a member of the Coastal Guard Company or its successors. Abel Miranda is not recorded as enlisting in the Confederate army until June 1, 1864 (Company F of the Second Infantry Battalion). After the raid, Miranda moved his family to Tampa. When the war ended, Miranda moved back to Pinellas, but not to Big Bayou. Instead, he relocated two miles inland, where he declared no "d__d Yankee" gunboat could reach.

Union troops remained garrisoned at Tampa after the war until 1869. Historian Walter P. Fuller wrote in 1971 that the Civil War "halted all growth in the St. Petersburg area for 15 years, impoverished the people, caused bitterness that in some quarters makes the event a touchy topic of conversation to this good day." The Civil War in Pinellas and the surrounding Tampa Bay was no Shiloh or Antietam, but to those who lived it there, it was just as brutal and deadly, for civilians and soldiers alike. Historian Fuller entitled the Civil War chapter in his book "Fratricide." That describes it well.

Sources used in this chapter include Ray Arsenault, *St. Petersburg and the Florida Dram: 1888–1950*; Rick Baker, *Mangroves to Major Leagues*; George Bartlett, "Skyline Changed by New Development," *St. Petersburg Times*; John A. Bethell, *Bethell's History of Pinellas Point*; Jefferson B. Browne, *Key West: The Old and the New*; Egmont Key Alliance, "An Island History"; Walter P. Fuller, *St. Petersburg and Its People*; Karl H. Grismer, *The Story of Pinellas*; *Official Records of the Union and Confederate Navies in the War of the Rebellion*, series I, vol. 17; Will Michaels, "Civil War in St. Pete?: Sesquicentennial," *Northeast Journal*, 2011; Zack C. Waters, "Tampa's Forgotten Defenders the Confederate Commanders of Fort Brooke," *Sunland Tribune*; Robert Watson, "Watson Diary: His Confederate Diary, Copied from original loaned by Mrs. Caroline Elizabeth (Watson) Hattrick," manuscript, 1861–62; *Gulf Beach News*, "Robert Watson: His Confederate War Diary," October 1, 1943; and consultation with Fritz Wilder and Jessie Marshall, Veterans Memorial Park.

Williams Park

Our Town Square

Before there was our celebrated Waterfront Park, there was Williams Park. It was named after John Constantine Williams, one of the three founders of our city. Williams Park was established in 1894, six years after the city was founded and platted. The land, a whole city block, was set aside by agreement between John C. Williams and Peter Demens in 1888 as part of the original town plat. From 1888 until 1893, the park remained in its frontier state, with oaks, pines and palmetto bushes. Early settler John Freeman Murphy even recalled shooting a deer and wild boar there. Mattie Lou Boswell Cherbonneaux described her first experience at the park around the turn of the last century: "My earliest memory of Williams Park was when Papa drove us to town in the surrey on business or other affairs. He would hitch the horse to a scrub oak tree. At that time the park was woods full of scrub oaks, patches of palmettos, pine trees, wax myrtle and other trees and bushes. There were cows grazing here and there." *St. Petersburg Times* editor William L. Straub described it as an "untrimmed jungle [and] convenient hiding place for truant boys and cows." Along the northern side of the park was a natural ditch that carried off the overflow waters from Mirror Lake. In its earliest days, it was mainly used for picnics.

In 1893, the Park Improvement Association was formed as a nongovernmental volunteer group. One of its members was Sarah Williams, John Williams's widow (John had died in 1892). A "Park Day" was declared by Mayor David Murray to clean up the park. A fence was built to keep out hogs and cattle. The first bandstand was erected in 1895. Later care for the park was taken over by the Woman's Town Improvement Association (WTIA), another voluntary organization. The WTIA president wrote about the group's park endeavors. Magnolias, water oaks and date palms were planted. "Little by little, Williams Park became a place of beauty...Walks were installed, a fountain installed in the center, benches scattered about." In 1910, the city assumed care of the park. In 1911, the city appointed its first park commissioner and appropriated significant funds for improving Williams Park.

A new bandstand was erected in 1920 at a cost of $10,000. John S. Silas was the contractor. The previous bandstand was moved to Waterfront Park, where it was soon destroyed in the 1921 hurricane. A replica of the original bandstand may be found at Heritage Park in Largo. It is frequently used as a wedding venue. In 1953, architect William Harvard Sr. erected the current bandstand. His avant-garde design won national awards, including the award of merit from the American Institute of Architects. The blue and green glass canopy, designed to provide shelter while letting in natural light, also received the Test of Time Award from the Florida Association of the American Institute of Architects. This radically different architecture from the previous band shell was not received without controversy by the public.

Originally, the park was simply called City Park. But some years later, as other parks were established throughout the city and given distinctive names, it was renamed after city founder John Williams. The park was to become the city's town square. Surrounding the park at its height were such buildings as First Methodist Church, St. Peter's Episcopal Church (later Cathedral), First Baptist Church, the Princess Martha Hotel, the open-air post office, the Women's Town Improvement Association's Headquarters, the Dennis Hotel and, much later, the Maas Brothers Department Store (now partially replaced by the new Progress Energy Building). Some of the city's finest architecture may be found among these buildings—Neoclassical, Florida Gothic, Gothic Revival, Beaux Arts and Mediterranean Revival.

The Sunshine Pleasure Club came to Williams Park in 1912, taking over the southeast corner. Horseshoes (known as "barnyard golf") and quoit lanes were laid out under the shade trees. Benches and tables were added for chess, checkers and dominos. Later, several croquet courts were built. These organized activities sponsored by local clubs became so popular that the park became overrun with people. In 1922, the John C. Williams family heirs objected to any club having exclusive rights to use any portion of the park and went to court over it. They contended that the park was given to the city with the understanding that it would be open to the public at

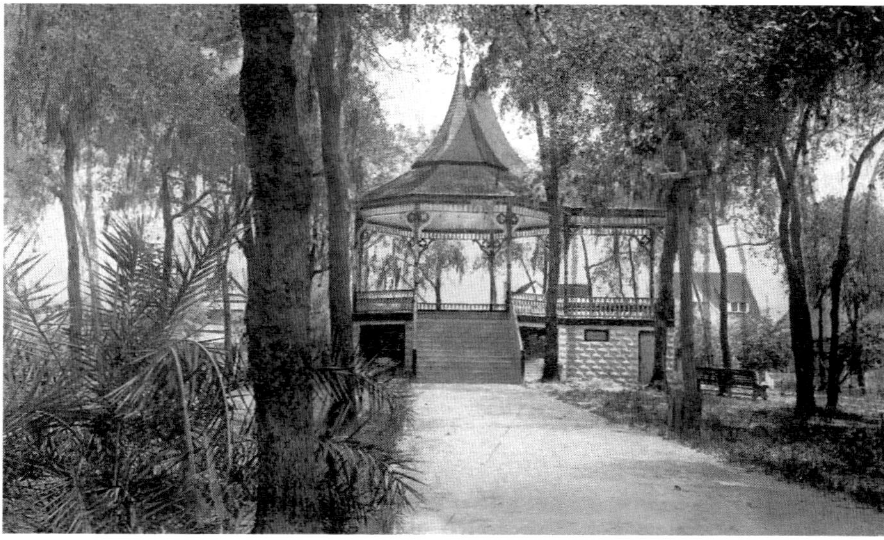

The first bandstand was erected in Williams Park in 1895. St. Petersburg Post Card Association. *Courtesy Michaels Family Collection.*

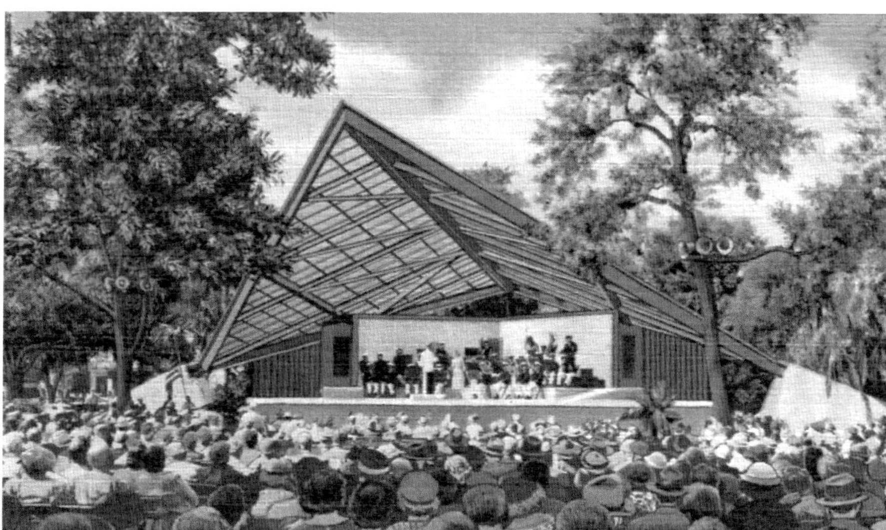

The current Williams Park band shell is an excellent example of modern mid-century architecture. The band shell was designed by William Harvard Sr. and constructed in 1953. Harvard also designed the Inverted Pyramid Pier building, the Central Library, Derby Lane and the Pasadena Community Church. Sun News Company. *Courtesy Michaels Family Collection.*

all times, and no individuals or groups should have special privileges. They were successful and got a court injunction to stop the Pleasure Club and other associations from using it. The injunction ended Williams Park's use as a sports center. Clubs using Williams Park moved on to Waterfront Park and Mirror Lake.

By 1913, the city's Board of Trade was sponsoring Sunday band concerts. The city engaged the Royal Scotch Highlanders Band to play in the park for the winters starting in 1917. The concerts helped to attract thousands of people during the winter months, and the park became famous throughout the country. It was also regularly used as a venue for city celebrations. In November 1918, some four to five thousand people gathered in Williams Park to celebrate the end of World War I. Billy Sunday preached there. Orson Wells is said to have spoken there as a child prodigy in about 1921. John Philip Sousa conducted there. The churches surrounding the park had Easter egg hunts and animal blessings. In 1924, the park was the site of a major celebration for the opening of the Gandy Bridge. In the 1930s, the comic actor Buster Keaton, who was making films at nearby Weedon Island, was presented with the key to the city in the park. African American children from Davis Academy performed singing and recitation programs there. In 1930, some ten thousand people were reported to attend a "soft-water jubilee" celebrating the city's new water system. In the 1960s, "love-ins" were held.

And then there were the political candidates. In 1906, Florida governor Napoleon Bonaparte Broward spoke there. Proponents of separating St. Petersburg and the Pinellas Peninsula from Hillsborough County staged a rally in 1908. Much later came presidents and vice presidents. These included Vice President Hubert Humphrey, President Richard Nixon, President Gerald Ford, President Ronald Reagan and Vice President George H.W. Bush. Jimmy Carter held a town hall meeting at the Princess Martha Hotel, across the street from the park. Some early political rallies were said to have attracted as many as 15,000 people. These headcounts appear to be enthusiastic exaggerations. Park officials estimate the park's capacity at about 4,500, without overflowing into the streets.

There is the story of one prominent political candidate who found his speech being interrupted by prolonged bell ringing at nearby St. Peter's Cathedral. Someone was sent to stop the ringing only to be told that a funeral was in progress, and the tradition of the church was to ring the bell once for each year of the seventy-year-old deceased's life. While this story is unsubstantiated, nearby First Methodist did initiate a carillon concert during a Reagan rally.

There are many memorials at the park. Of course, there is a historic marker for John C. Williams himself. Interestingly, this was erected by the Princess Hirrihigua Chapter of the Daughters of the American Revolution in 1936. (This was the princess who saved Pánfilo de Narváez expedition survivor Juan Ortiz from being burned at the stake.) A war memorial was erected after World War I by the American War Mothers to commemorate those city residents who died in the "Great War." The inscription reads, "God gave us sons. We gave them to our country, and our country gave them back to God." There are names of sixteen soldiers, including two African Americans. The word "colored" is affixed after the names of the latter. Historian Raymond Arsenault wrote that this suffix provided "future generations with a haunting reminder that the city of sunshine was also the city of shadow."

Later monuments were added for World War II, Korean War and Vietnam War veterans. There is one for merchant seamen. There is a full-size statute commemorating Polish Revolutionary War hero Thaddeus Kosciuszko, erected by the American Institute of Polish Culture. Another memorial is for William A. Kenman for bringing "keen enjoyment and clean entertainment" to the bandstand of the park. There is one for former city councilman Horace Williams Jr. A small memorial was erected in 1980 to celebrate Esther Wright, renown as the "Bird Lady of St. Petersburg." In addition to the pigeons in the park, she fed thousands of birds and many stray cats throughout downtown.

Sources used in this chapter include Raymond Arsenault, *St. Petersburg and the Florida Dream, 1888–1950*; Rick Baker, *Mangroves to Major League: A Timeline of St. Petersburg, Florida*; Walter P. Fuller, *St. Petersburg and Its People*; Rita Slaght Gould, *Pioneer St. Petersburg*; Karl H. Grismer, *The Story of St. Petersburg*; Scott Taylor Hartzell, *Remembering St. Petersburg, Florida*, vols. 1 and 2; Will Michaels, "Williams Park: Our Town Square," *Northeast Journal*, 2009; *St. Petersburg Times*; and communication with Marilyn Olsen, president of the Downtown Neighborhood Association.

St. Petersburg's Piers

Anchor of the Downtown

St. Petersburg's most celebrated landmark is its pier, now with the Inverted Pyramid Pier building at its head. The city's first pier was the Railroad Pier at the foot of First Avenue South, for a long time also called Railroad Avenue. This pier was built in 1889 by one of the city's three founders, the Russian Peter Demens. The other founders were John C. Williams and his wife, Sarah. The pier was three thousand feet long and was soon lined with loading docks and warehouses. Despite its length, the water depth at the terminus was only twelve feet in shallow Tampa Bay. The railroad traveled out on this pier to connect its cargo with docking freight ships. Along with other early town builders, Demens and his Orange Belt Railway also sought to promote tourism. A large bathing pavilion was built attached to the Railroad Pier for the use of tourists, and fishing was encouraged.

The Railroad Pier eventually was taken over by the Henry B. Plant's Sanford and St. Petersburg Railroad, successor to Peter Demens's Orange Belt Railway. Plant and his associates exercised what amounted to a monopoly on major shipping in St. Petersburg. In 1901, the owners of the passenger steamer *Anthea* decided to deepen the channel to their Central Avenue dock. Concerned that a new channel would weaken their commercial position, the directors of the Plant System obtained an injunction blocking the deepening of the channel. This action enraged the local business community, which countered with a plan to terminate the Railroad Pier's monopoly. Led by A.P. Avery, a former baker turned banker, the businessmen dredged a T-shaped channel that would open the shoreline between Central and First Avenue

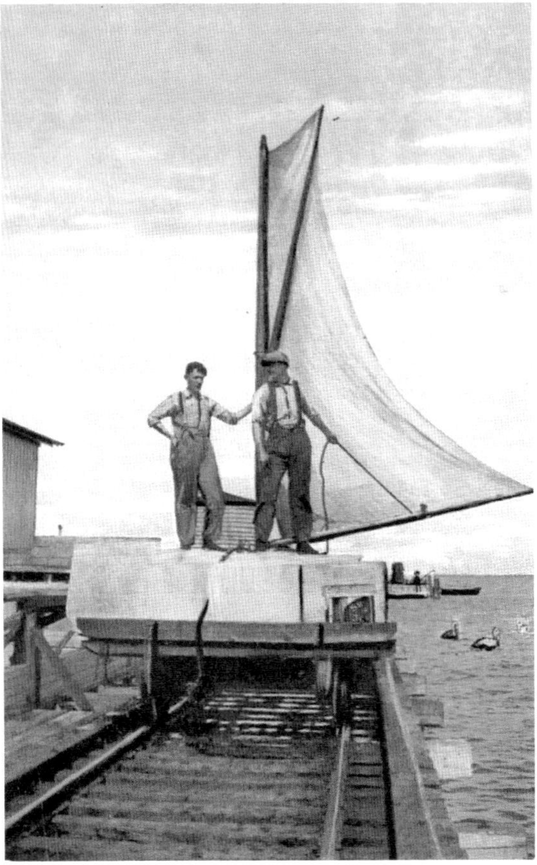

Small railroad sail car rigged with a sail to run ice up to the fish warehouses on the Railroad Pier. The sail car operated from 1893 until 1912, when a winter visitor was accidently killed. St. Petersburg Post Card Association. *Courtesy Michaels Family Collection.*

North to deep-draft vessels leading to a small dock at the end of Central Avenue. B.E. Coe did the dredging, and the channel was therefore known as the Little Coe Channel.

From 1896 to 1926

The present pier at the foot of Second Avenue Northeast evolved over three periods. The first period (1896–1926) began with a 1,500-foot pier built by D.F.S. Brantley. The Brantley Pier was built as an alternative to H.B. Plant's Railroad Pier. At its terminus, the water depth was a mere 7 feet. A small

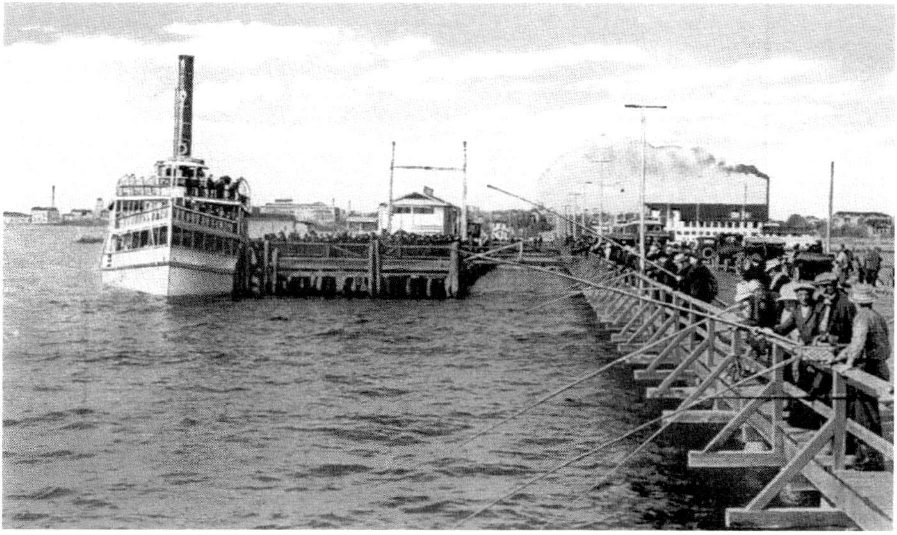

Postcard view of the Brantley Pier. The Brantley was succeeded by the Electric Pier in 1906, named for its hundreds of electric lights. The Electric Pier was operated by F.A. Davis, owner of the electric power company and trolley system. *Courtesy Michaels Family Collection.*

horse-drawn flatcar was used to carry passengers from off-loading ships to the shore. It also included a thirty-four-room bathing pavilion some 1,000 feet from the shore. The Brantley Pier was succeeded by the Electric Pier in 1906, named for its hundreds of incandescent lights. This pier was 3,000 feet long and 16 feet wide. The pier's owner was F.A. Davis, who operated both the city's power plant and trolley line. In addition to stringing the pier with electric lights powered by his plant, he also ran a trolley down the length of the pier. This became a major tourist attraction. In 1913, the Municipal Recreation Pier was built by the city alongside the Electric Pier. The Electric Pier was torn down in 1914.

FROM 1926 TO 1971

While the Municipal Recreation Pier was repaired after the 1921 hurricane, city engineers warned that it would need to be soon replaced. Consequently, Lew Brown, editor of the *Evening Independent* newspaper, championed

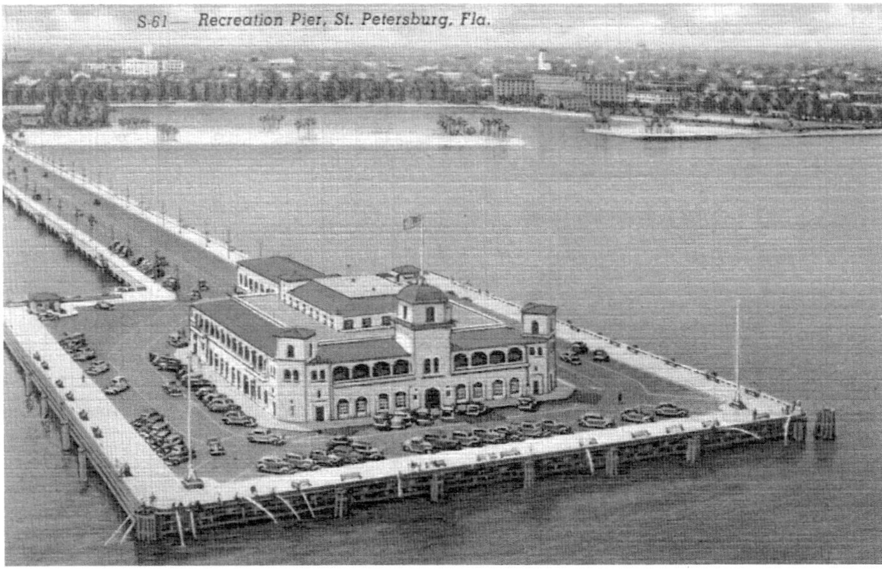

Million Dollar Pier with roof, 1926. The pier head boasted twelve thousand square feet of space. Sun News Company, St. Petersburg. Postcard dated 1943. *Courtesy Michaels Family Collection.*

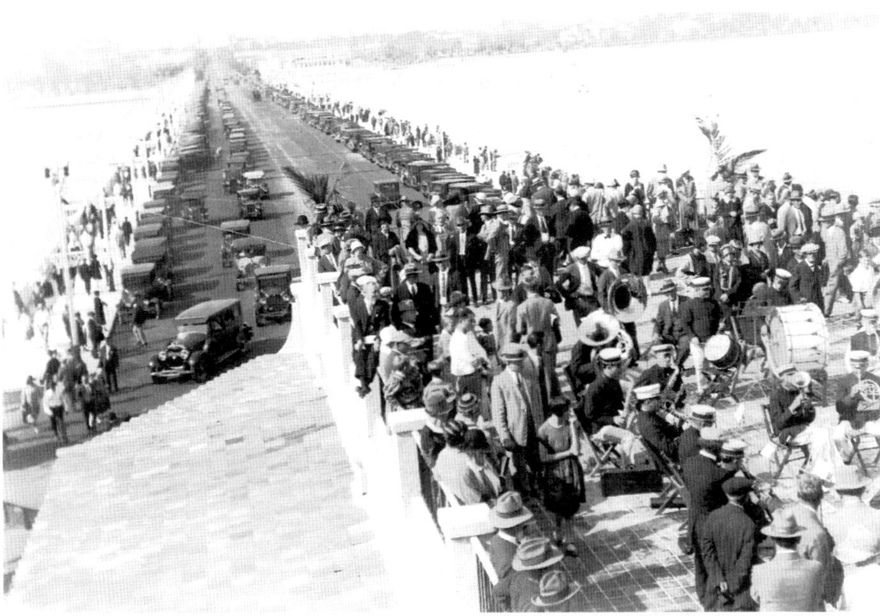

Dedication of the Million Dollar Pier, November 29, 1926. *Courtesy Michaels Family Collection.*

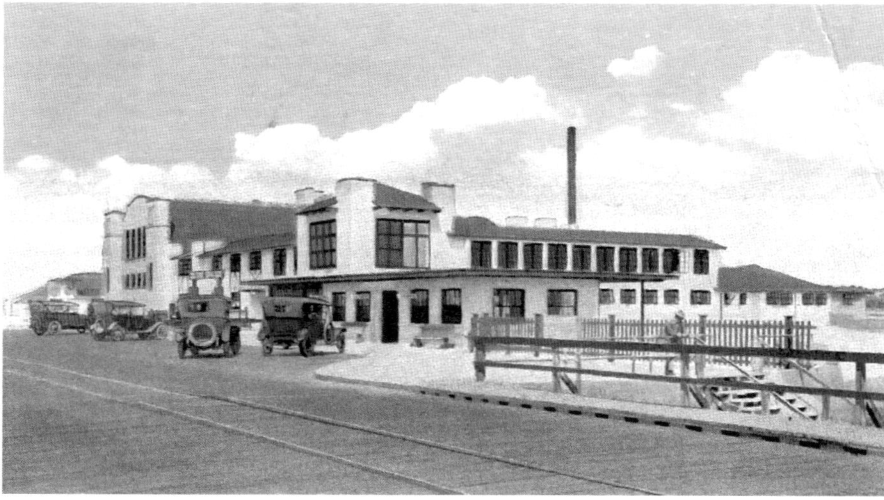

Just three years after the establishment of Waterfront Park, the Spa and Municipal Pier were built. William L. Straub called the Spa "splendid" and expected it to "pay substantial revenue to the city." *Courtesy Michaels Family Collection.*

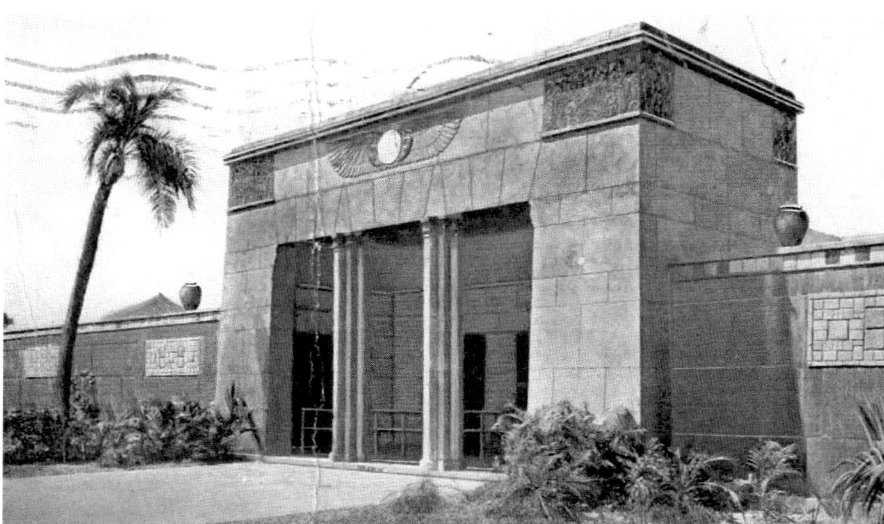

The Municipal Solarium was built on the pier approach in 1930 by the city at a cost of $15,000. Straub's *St. Petersburg Times* lauded the "medicinal benefits" of sunbathing and enthusiastically endorsed city government's investment in the project. The reverse of the postcard advertises "an institution devoted exclusively to heliotherapy and is modern in every respect…St. Petersburg Prescription: 'Ultra-violet rays. Dose: A Little Every Day.'" Asheville Post Card Company, Asheville, North Carolina. Postcard dated 1935. *Courtesy Michaels Family Collection.*

replacing it with a bigger and better pier. This was known as the "Million Dollar Pier" because that is almost what it cost the city to build—$998,729.18 to be exact. Lew Brown obtained $300,000.00 in private pledges toward construction of the new pier, and the city council proposed a $1 million bond issue approved by the voters in 1925.

An elaborate Mediterranean Revival–style building called the Casino was built at the pier head and completed in 1926. This style of architecture was cutting edge for its time. It soon became St. Petersburg's signature architecture, although bungalows (especially in residential areas) ran a close second. The new pier was 1,452 feet long, including the head, and 100 feet wide along the bridge. Despite the Casino's name, no gambling was allowed. The pier was dedicated on Thanksgiving Day before a crowd of ten thousand. The Casino originally boasted an open-air ballroom where three thousand couples danced on the first night. As historian Ray Arsenault stated, many of those couples wondered if the "Florida Dream" could ever get any better than this. The Pier Casino also included a central atrium for streetcars and an observation deck. Beginning in 1927, the radio studio of WSUN was located there. Piper-Fuller Airport was dedicated the same day as the pier. This was the city's first airport, located in what is now the Tyrone area, the general site of Tyrone Square Mall. The city had purchased land for the airport from R.L. Piper of Tyrone, Pennsylvania, and Walter P. Fuller, a St. Petersburg entrepreneur and later historian.

FROM 1973 TO 2012

In 1967, the Million Dollar Pier Casino building at the pier's head was demolished and replaced by the current inverted pyramid design in 1973. The one-hundred-foot-wide bridge leading out to the head was not replaced. The Inverted Pyramid Pier was intended to be an icon, similar to a lighthouse. It was designed so that there would be minimal interruption of the view of the bay from the shoreline. The first floor of the pyramid was later enlarged, masking some of the view and reducing the amount of deck space. It was planned for an observation deck on the roof, a restaurant on the fourth floor, community meeting rooms and activity space on the third floor, St. Petersburg Chamber of Commerce space on the second floor and a lobby and deck area on the first floor. The greatest occupancy was intended to be

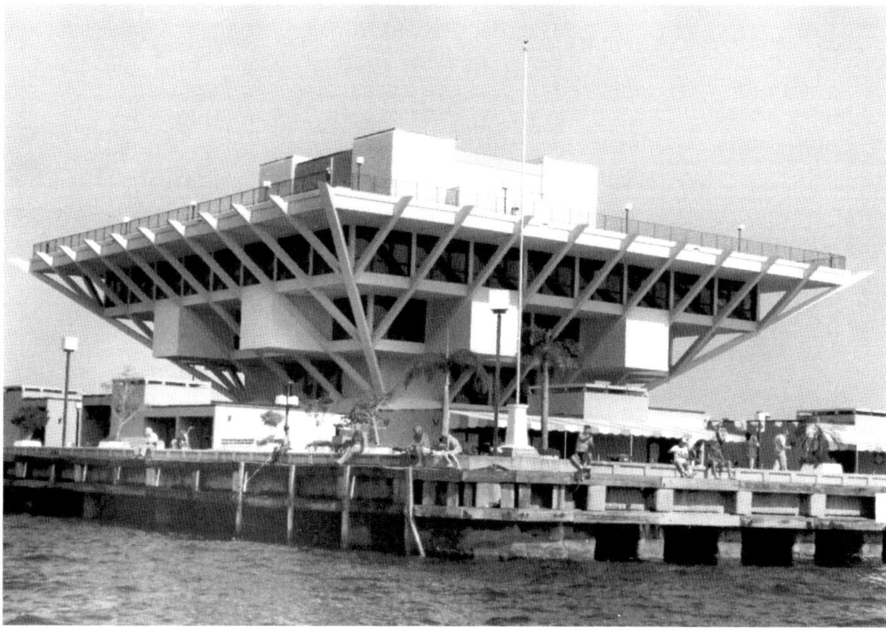

The Inverted Pyramid Pier building was designed by architect William Harvard Sr. and was opened in 1973. The architecture was a sharp departure from the previous Million Dollar Pier, built in the Mediterranean Revival style. The original design did not include the buildings on the first level surrounding the inverted pyramid. *Courtesy Michaels Family Collection.*

at the top, where views would be best. Retail space was considered ancillary and to be provided in kiosks surrounding the first floor. Functionally, the building was designed to minimize the mass of the foundation required to support a four-story building.

The pyramid's architect was William Harvard Sr. Harvard was a leading city architect influenced by the Bauhaus school of design and architects such as Mies van der Rohe and Frank Lloyd Wright. Other works by Harvard are the 1953 band shell at William's Park, Pasadena Community Church, the Central Library, Derby Lane and the Federal Building (now demolished). The Inverted Pyramid Pier is city owned, as was its predecessor, the Million Dollar Pier.

The present pier, simply called "The Pier," including the bridge leading out to the inverted pyramid head, is now coming to the end of its life cycle. The Inverted Pyramid was a very controversial design at the time it was built. Over the years, it has grown in popularity and has, in many ways, become more than just a striking visual symbol of the city—it has become its effective logo. Anyone who has watched a major city sports event on TV has probably seen the Inverted Pyramid Pier when scans are shown of the city. The pier and the Waterfront Parks have always been an important part of St. Petersburg's sense of place, for residents and visitors alike. Many residents have strong, personal emotional attachments to the waterfront. In 2012, some twenty thousand citizens signed a petition to save the Inverted Pyramid Pier from the wrecking ball. Plans for a new pier have been proposed and are being passionately debated.

Sources used in this chapter include Raymond Arsenault, *St. Petersburg and the Florida Dream, 1888–1950*; Rick Baker, *Mangroves to Major League: A Timeline of St. Petersburg, Florida*; Walter P. Fuller, *St. Petersburg and Its People*; Karl H. Grismer, *The Story of St. Petersburg*; Scott Taylor Hartzell, *Remembering St. Petersburg, Florida*, vol. 2; *Voices of America: St. Petersburg*; Will Michaels, "St. Petersburg's Piers: Anchor of the Downtown," *Northeast Journal*, 2008; St. Petersburg, Florida, *Solarium Spa Pool and Beach and Recreation Pier* pamphlet; St. Petersburg, Florida, *How to Use Your Pier* pamphlet; and the *St. Petersburg Times*.

The Fountain of Youth Rediscovered?

We have all heard of Ponce de Leon and the Fountain of Youth. According to legend, the Spanish explorer Juan Ponce de Leon was searching for a Fountain of Youth when he landed somewhere on the east coast of Florida in 1513. While the Fountain is believed to have been in the vicinity of St. Augustine, a variation of the story notes that it actually was located at Warm Mineral Springs in Port Charlotte. It was in today's Port Charlotte area that Ponce de Leon was mortally wounded by Calusa Indians in 1521.

But wait, maybe Ponce did not travel far enough in his search for the Fountain. About seventy miles north of Warm Mineral Springs is another Fountain of Youth in St. Petersburg. Perhaps these particular waters would have even cured Ponce of his mortal wound.

Tomlinson's Pier

Edwin H. Tomlinson began visiting St. Petersburg in 1891 and began to live here permanently about 1900. Before long, he was busy improving the city with a new palatial residence, churches, schools, parades, youth orchestras,

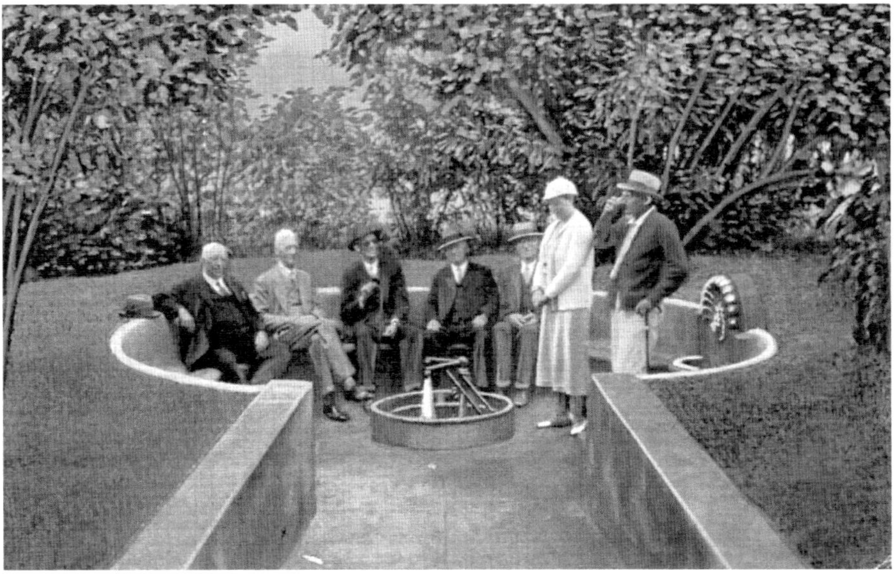

Early postcard of the keyhole-shaped Fountain of Youth. This fountain was located near Third Avenue South on Waterfront Park. E.C. Robison, St. Petersburg, image circa 1920s. *Courtesy Michaels Family Collection.*

a new open-air post office and a new pier located near the foot of Third Avenue South built in 1900. At the far end of the pier was a cottage that he built for his father, Peter. The cottage provided shelter for his father while he fished the bay through a hole in the floor. Near the entrance to the pier, he drilled a very sulfuric artesian well dubbed the "Fountain of Youth." Local historian Scott Hartzell has championed Edwin Tomlinson as one of the unsung heroes of St. Petersburg.

Artesian wells are bored to such great depths through a permeable rock layer that the water pressure forces the water to the surface. There is no need for a pump. The name is derived from the French region of Artois, site of the oldest known well in Europe. The water in Tomlinson's Fountain contained a large amount of sulfur that could be smelled a block away. Tomlinson promoted the Fountain as having nearly miraculous restorative powers. For years, people went there daily with jars and jugs to get the coveted water. In 1971, it was determined that the water contained more lithium than any other spring in Pinellas County. Lithium is used as a mood stabilizer. Small wonder it was so popular.

DR. CONRAD

In 1908, a visitor to St. Petersburg by the name of Dr. Jesse F. Conrad sampled the water at the Fountain and thought that the Tomlinson Pier might be a good place for a spa. Upon returning home to Ohio, he joked that if William Howard Taft was elected president, he would return to St. Petersburg and buy the Tomlinson Pier. It turned out that Taft was elected, and Conrad was not joking. He went back to St. Petersburg and bought the pier. He embellished the entrance with an arch made of willow branches and sold dips in the sulfur water bath and drinks from the spring.

MORE RECENT HISTORY

When the Tomlinson Pier was destroyed in the 1921 hurricane, the Fountain of Youth was moved to a park at Third Avenue South. In 1946, it was again moved to Progress Energy Park/Al Lang Field, at Fourth Avenue South and First Street Southeast. In the beginning, it was a humble affair: a small keyhole-shaped area with a low basin in the middle. Later, it was enlarged, and a squared entryway was added with a sign proclaiming "Fountain of Youth" at the top. Still later, a statue of Ponce de Leon graced the center of a now raised fountain. This was then replaced with a blue-green maiden. Now that, too, is gone, replaced with a pair of lion's heads in relief on the walls facing the Fountain. The original footprint of the site has shrunk in size. At one time, water for the Fountain was piped in from Tomlinson's artesian well. Then, for a long while, there was no water at all. Today, the Fountain spouts just plain tap water. It has no smell and no lithium either.

FOUNTAIN REDISCOVERED?

What happened to Tomlinson's original artesian well? Some think that it has been recently rediscovered in the south yacht basin east of the boat slips. A four-inch diameter pipe protrudes about three feet from the bottom of the bay, at a depth of about thirteen feet. Brackish water still flows. Its temperature is about eighty degrees—twelve degrees warmer than the surrounding waters of the bay. And this warmer water attracts manatees. More research is needed to fully establish this well as Tomlinson's. The Fountain of Youth became a focus of attention again in 2008 when the Ray's baseball team owners proposed relocating Tropicana Stadium to the waterfront. Some expressed concern that the possible Fountain of Youth well in the yacht basin and the monument located at Fourth Avenue South might be displaced. The Fountain of Youth continues to make history. Ponce and Tomlinson would be amazed.

Sources used in this chapter include Raymond Arsenault, *St. Petersburg and the Florida Dream, 1888–1950*; Rick Baker, *Mangroves to Major League: A Timeline of St. Petersburg, Florida*; Karl H. Grismer, *History of St. Petersburg*; Scott Taylor Hartzell, *Remembering St. Petersburg*; *St. Petersburg Times*; Will Michaels, "Fountain of Youth Rediscovered," *Northeast Journal*, 2008; Southwest Florida Water Management District, *Submarine Springs and Other Karst Features in Offshore Waters of the Gulf of Mexico and Tampa Bay*; the *Tampa Tribune*; communication from Tampa Bay Rays Baseball senior vice-president Michael Kalt; and assistance from Bruce Olsen, member of Saint Petersburg Preservation.

William L. Straub

Father of Our Waterfront Parks

One of our city's greatest assets, perhaps the greatest, is our downtown Waterfront Parks. They are one of the city's most striking visual symbols. The first Waterfront Park ranged from about Fourth Avenue South to Fifth Avenue North. Now they stretch from Poynter Park adjacent to the old Dali Museum building on the south to Coffee Pot Park on the north. They cover about seven linear miles and more than one hundred acres. Included within this area are now fifteen parks: Poynter Park, Albert Whitted Park, Al Lang Field, Pioneer Park, Demens Landing, South Straub Park (also called Soreno Park), North Straub Park, Spa Beach, Vinoy Park, North Shore Park, Elva Rouse Park (including the Gizella Kopsick Palm Arboretum), Flora Wylie Park, Coffee Pot Boulevard and Granada Terrace and Northeast Exchange Coffee Pot Park.

From earliest times, the downtown waterfront was a mix of commercial and recreational use. Along with other early town builders, Peter Demens and his railroad sought to promote tourism in addition to shipping. A large bathing pavilion was added to the Railroad Pier for the use of tourists in 1890.

The editor of the *St. Petersburg Times*, William L. Straub, was not enthusiastic about the dredging of the Coe Channel. While Straub favored the expansion of the city's port facilities, he was also worried that expansion would destroy the potential beauty of the downtown waterfront. Straub was also an artist who appreciated the natural beauty of the bay. He was equally concerned that further commercialization of the waterfront could negatively affect the growing tourist trade. The waterfront was already becoming

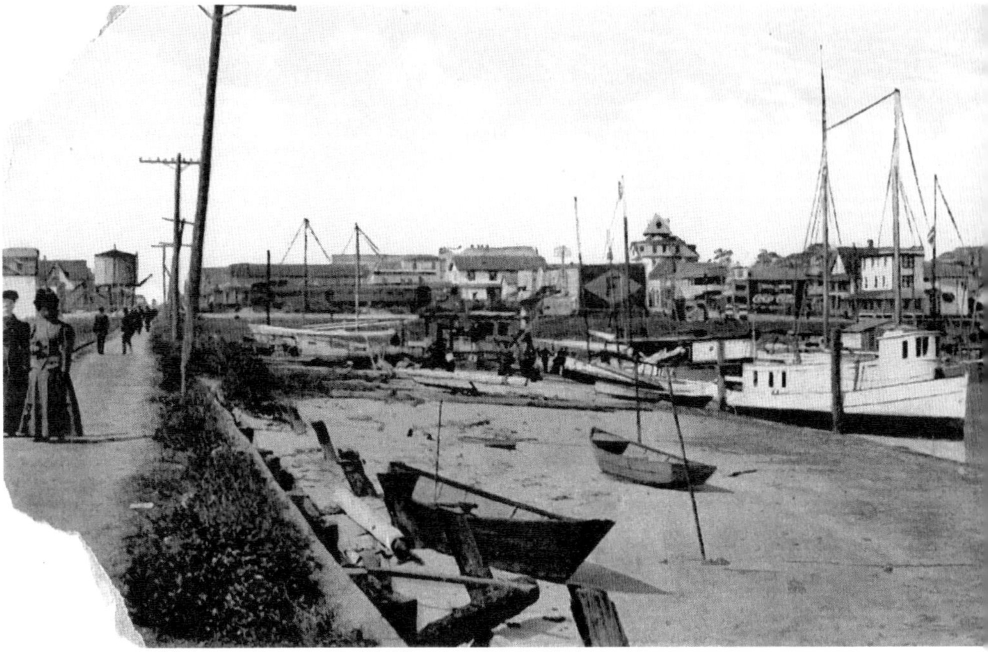

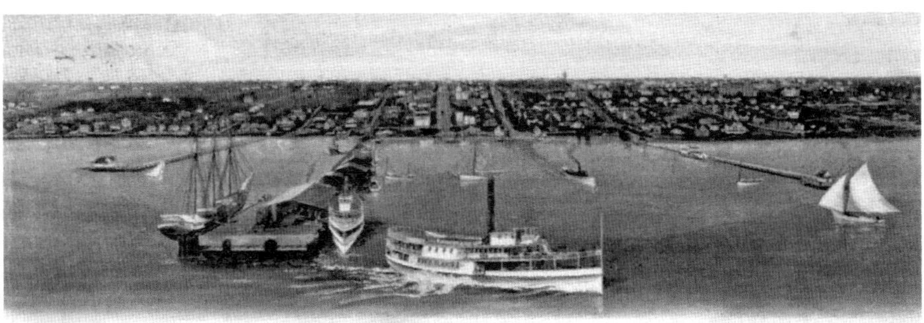

Above: Panoramic view of the waterfront as imagined by *St. Petersburg Times* editor William L. Straub in 1903. Straub was an accomplished artist as well as a cartoonist, newspaper editor and publisher. The painting was made for his friend F.A. Davis, owner of the electric power company, the trolley system and the Electric Pier. The original painting hangs in the *Tampa Bay Times* building. Rotograph Company, New York. Postcard dated 1909. *Courtesy Michaels Family Collection.*

Top: Very early panoramic view of the waterfront taken from the Railroad Pier before creation of the Waterfront Parks. The electric power company is on the right with the two smokestacks. The Detroit Hotel is the tall building in the background, and note that the Coca-Cola sign is in the foreground. *Courtesy Michaels Family Collection.*

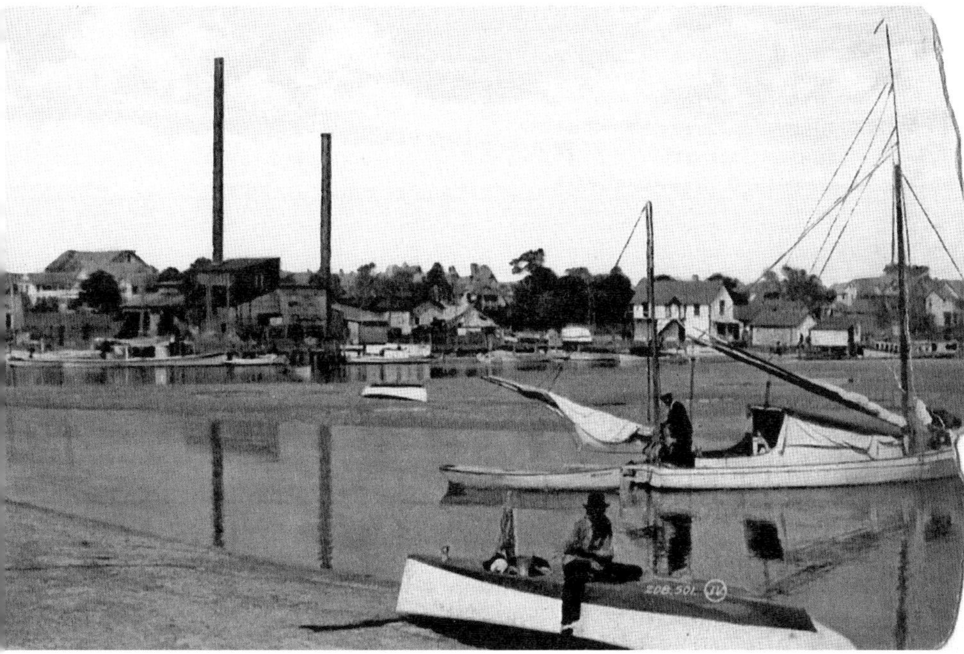

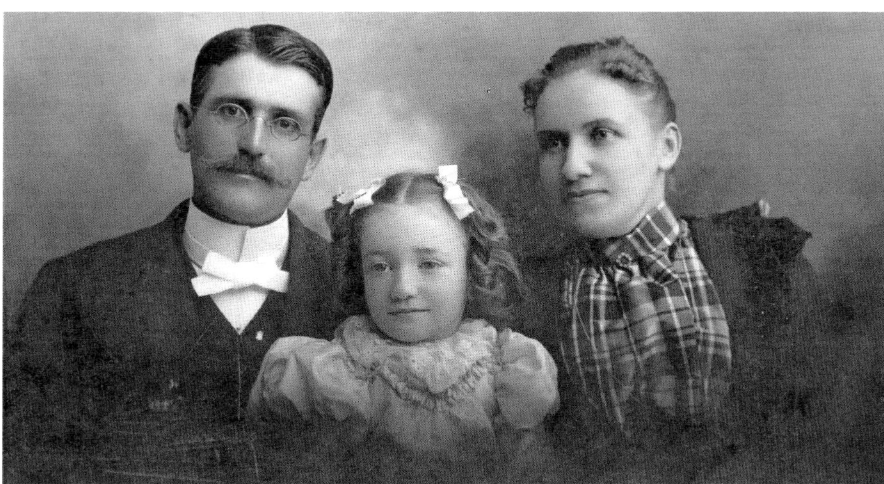

William and Sarah Straub with their daughter, Blanche, in 1899. The dredge used to dig the waterfront yacht basin was named the *Blanche* in recognition of Straub's work to secure the downtown waterfront for public use. *Courtesy St. Petersburg Museum of History*.

littered with unkempt docks and smelly fish processing houses. There also was F.A. Davis's electric power plant, with two tall smoking stacks.

At one point, the Board of Trade issued a report declaring:

> *We found that nearly the whole water front was in an insanitary and unsightly condition—decaying seaweed and other vegetable, as well as animal matter, produced obnoxious odors, rendering residence along the front almost intolerable and beyond all question detrimental to health... The general appearance of decay and neglect between the two docks—old boats, rotting piers, all sorts of riff-raff, and especially where the outgoing tide leaves large stretches of sand covered with a variety of animal and vegetable matter in all stages of decay—does not well comport with a live, progressive city such as St. Petersburg claims to be.*

A struggle ensued between various business and civic interests over whether the downtown waterfront was to become primarily a commercial port or a waterfront park for use of tourists and as an amenity for adjacent residential neighborhoods. Straub's eventual solution was to preserve the downtown waterfront by promoting C.A. Harvey's proposed port farther south at Bayboro, in the vicinity of Tenth Avenue South. A commercial port was, in fact, developed there and prospered for many years. This site is now primarily the location of the University of South Florida St. Petersburg, although the Coast Guard also still has a facility there, small cruise ships have docked there from time to time and there is a marina.

Debate over the waterfront park began in 1902 after the Board of Trade approved a resolution calling for a public bay-front park between Second and Fifth Avenues North. Straub backed the resolution through editorials in the *Times*. But the first real advance of the park vision occurred in 1905 when J.M. Lewis presented a plan to turn virtually the entire downtown waterfront into a park. Lewis's plan became a major issue in the 1906 city elections, and the public waterfront supporters eventually won a majority of the seats on the city council. In February 1906, a waterfront owner planned to build a number of rental cottages on the waterfront. Concerned that this would unleash a spate of low-end rental units on the waterfront, the city responded by passing an ordinance that ordered no buildings other than boathouses or bathing pavilions were to be built on the waterfront unless approved by the city. In April, the Board of Trade, under the leadership of C. Perry Snell, who developed residential neighborhoods in northeast St. Petersburg and later Snell Isle, began to buy up waterfront property and hold it in trust until the city could afford to turn the property into parkland.

The struggle continued. In 1908, the newly elected city council was opposed to the waterfront park. At that point, waterfront boosters formed the St. Petersburg Waterfront Company for the purpose of taking over the waterfront lots previously purchased, acquiring the remaining property, creating a yacht basin, providing for commercial traffic to the south and beautifying the park. Creation of this company suddenly sparked the city council to action. The council and a group of public ownership advocates secured money to buy the waterfront lots previously purchased by the Board of Trade for public ownership, with the first deed dated January 8, 1909. All the remaining waterfront property, except that held by the Atlantic Coast Line Railroad and the electric light company, was obtained by the Board of Trade in December 1909. Final arrangement were made on Christmas Eve and resulted in what Straub's *Times* called "the best Christmas present that St. Petersburg ever had."

Five months later, the dredge *Blanche*, named in honor of Blanche Straub, W.L. Straub's daughter, began work on the waterfront improvements. Waterfront Park finally became an official park in December 1910. In 1911, seawalls were added. By 1916, St. Petersburg had one of the largest public waterfronts in the nation. By 1925, the total public cost of purchasing and improving the waterfront had come to almost $2 million.

Historian Walter P. Fuller stated that in 1908 and 1909, the waterfront between Second Avenue North and First Avenue South was the scene of a "fierce struggle" between William Straub and F.A. Davis. Davis was an early city booster and entrepreneur who began his activities in St. Petersburg in 1897 when he founded the city's first electric light company. In 1902, he began the city's first trolley line. Before coming to Florida, he was a successful Philadelphia publisher, and he used his publishing company to promote investment and tourism in St. Petersburg across the nation. He also successfully encouraged many Philadelphia financial interests, including Jacob Disston (brother of Hamilton Disston, who founded Gulfport) and George S. Gandy, to invest in his St. Petersburg enterprises.

In 1906, Davis formed the Tampa Bay Transportation Company. In May of that year, the *Philadelphia North American* newspaper reported, "Capitalists in Philadelphia plan to make St. Petersburg one of the most important ports in the South Atlantic States." It was planned to develop St. Petersburg as a port for West Indian, Gulf and South American trade, as well as to be ready for heavier commerce by the time the Panama Canal was completed. In that

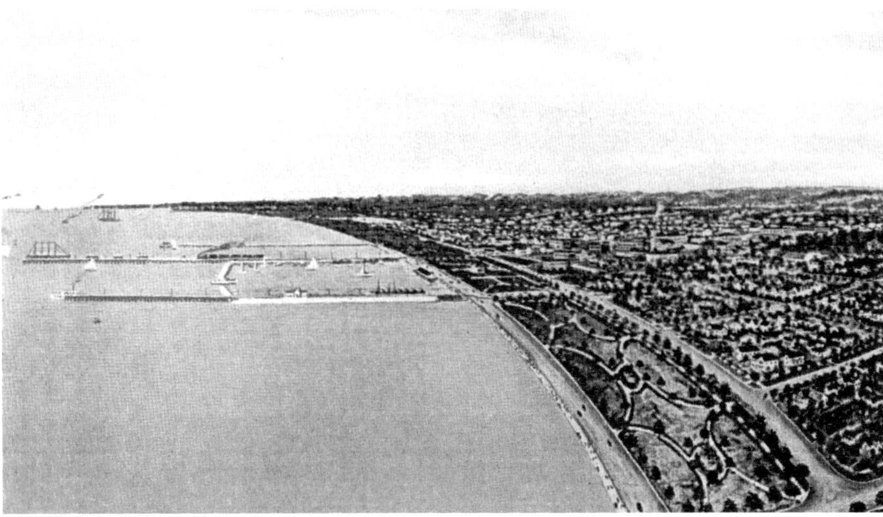

Very early postcard imagining the Waterfront Park "now in course of construction." The postcard depicts three piers—the Electric Pier, the Railroad Pier and the Tomlinson/Fountain of Youth Pier. *Courtesy Michaels Family Collection.*

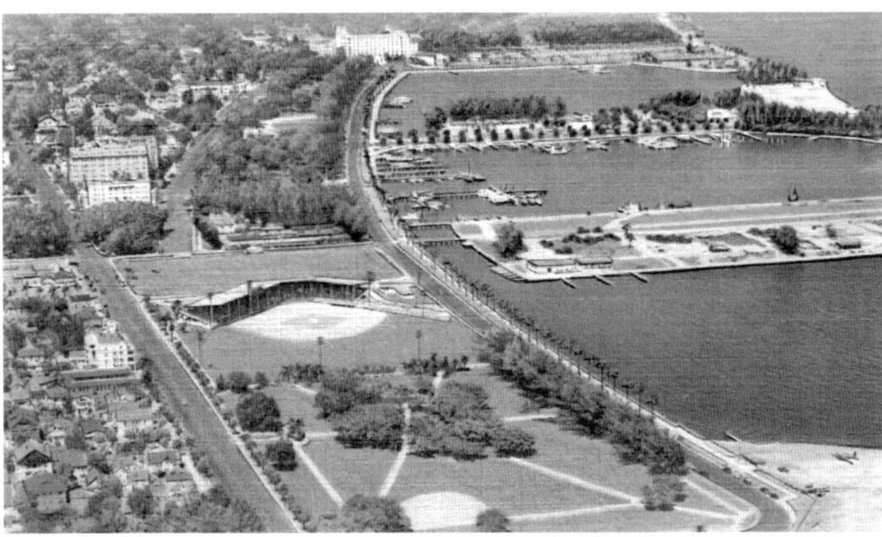

Waterfront Park as viewed from the south, with Fountain of Youth, Kids and Cubs Three-Quarter Century Club Field, Al Lang Field, yacht basins and Vinoy Park Hotel (at top). Al Lang Field was first built in 1947 and was later replaced in 1977. This photo shows the 1947 stadium. Tichnor Bros. Incorporated, Boston. *Courtesy Michaels Family Collection.*

same year, another Davis company, the St. Petersburg Investment Company, acquired the Brantley Pier and extended it two thousand feet out to deep water. Davis decorated the pier with electric lights powered by his light company, and consequently the pier came to be known as the "Electric Pier."

Davis's intention was to make this the commercial freight pier for St. Petersburg. Freight was to be unloaded from boats on to freight cars that had wheels the same gauge as the city trolleys. The freight could then be easily transported to anywhere there were trolley rails. According to historian Karl Grismer, for many years the Electric Pier was the "deep water harbor" of the city. It also served as the recreation pier. In the wintertime, it swarmed with tourist anglers. Davis brought the SS *Favorite* to the Electric Pier to transport both freight and passengers. This ship is in many historic waterfront photos and in a painting done by Straub. At the time, it was the largest ship on Tampa Bay. If Davis really expected the opening of the Panama Canal to accelerate shipping on Tampa Bay, he was ahead of his time. The canal was not completed until 1914, only to be closed again the next year as the result of a giant landslide. The canal was not officially opened until 1920.

By the end of 1909, the city had purchased all of the original waterfront property except that held by the ACL Railroad and the Electric Light & Power Company. In 1911, the ACL leased its property to the city. The site of the Electric Light & Power Company, at the foot of Central Avenue, was acquired about 1914. This site was later leased by the city to the St. Petersburg Yacht Club for one dollar a year. The final piece of waterfront property at the foot of the Electric Pier was acquired by the city in 1919.

It is difficult to sort out the relationship between Straub and Davis, as well as the details of Davis's role in the Waterfront Park story. So far, we are unable to find a direct statement from Davis himself about the issue. While initially opposing Davis's request for a trolley franchise, Straub later served as secretary of Davis's trolley company. Certainly through 1906, the year Davis built the Electric Pier, Davis was actively pursuing commercial development of at least his part of the waterfront. But in the following year, 1907, a financial panic hit the Tampa Bay area, and Davis's enterprises collapsed. All of his companies were placed in receivership. According to historian Walter Fuller, at that point "Davis dropped from the St. Petersburg story."

Upon the occasion of F.A. Davis's death in 1917, Straub referred to Davis as a "dear friend." After reviewing all that Davis had achieved for the city, he stated that if any person should receive the honor of being called the "Father of St. Petersburg," it was Davis. While some may debate this title, there is little doubt that William L. Straub should be regarded as the "Father of

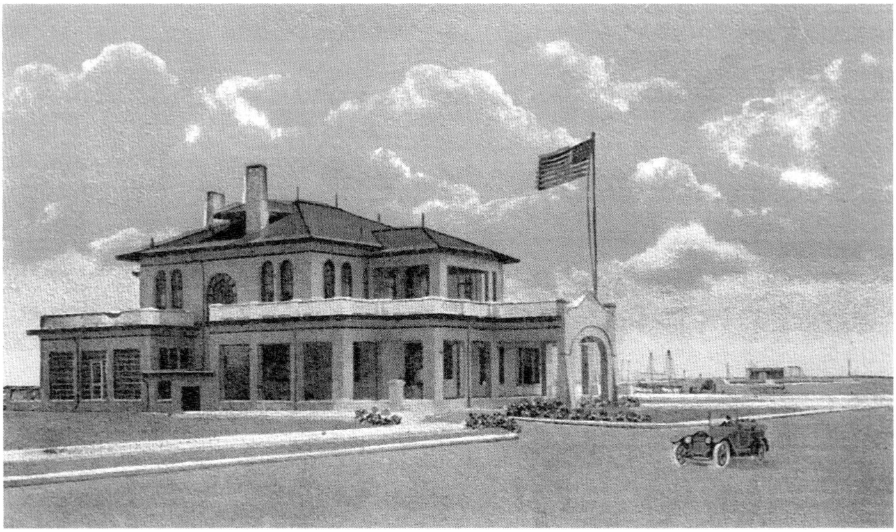

The St. Petersburg Yacht Club building dates from 1917. William L. Straub served as the first secretary of the yacht club. E.C. Kropp Company, Milwaukee. Postcard dated 1923. *Courtesy Michaels Family Collection.*

Our Waterfront Parks." Straub's championship of preserving the downtown waterfront for parkland was a bold action. Prime waterfront property was removed from the immediate tax rolls. But in the long run, this resulted in a better quality of life for our people, including a strong city economy based on tourism and residential development.

William Straub left his stamp on our city in more ways than just the Waterfront Parks. He campaigned for better roads and sidewalks, better public schools, a more humane penal system, a city-manager style government and the creation of the first public Parks Board. He was instrumental in bringing about the creation of Pinellas County, breaking it off from Hillsborough County (1912). It was not just *what* he did for our city but the *way* in which he did it. He pushed for positive change but brought it about in a manner that allowed for reasonable compromise and mutual respect. In 1902, he probably saved the lives of the officers of a failed bank when they became the targets of angry depositors. He helped to mediate a dispute over the incorporation of our city in 1903. He obtained the support of Clearwater for creation of Pinellas County by not insisting the county seat be located in St. Petersburg, even though St. Petersburg was much larger. In the words of his great-grandson, Frank Straub Starkey, "He was and continues to be a model of civic responsibility for us all."

As historian Walter P. Fuller put it, "Straub was the greatest influence for the development of the community ever to appear on the scene." He also had a special appreciation of St. Petersburg's sense of place, perhaps influenced in particular by his appreciation of art.

Resources used in this chapter include Raymond Arsenault, *St. Petersburg and the Florida Dream: 1888–1950*; Rick Baker, *Mangroves to Major League: A Timeline of St. Petersburg, Florida*; William C. Ballard, ed., *A Nautical Heritage—The St. Petersburg Yacht Club Story: 1909–2009*; Walter P. Fuller, *St. Petersburg and Its People*; Karl H. Grismer, *The Story of St. Petersburg*; Will Michaels, "William L. Straub: Father of Our Waterfront Parks," *Northeast Journal*, 2005; Will Michaels, "William Straub's Waterfront Revisited," *Northeast Journal*, 2010; *St. Petersburg Times* (particularly November 7, 1912; March 15, 1913; October 4, 1913, page 4; October 9, 1913, page 4; December 12, 1913, page 1; September 17, 1914, page 7; July 9, 1916, page 2; May 16, 1920, page 6; July 16, 1921, page 8; November 4, 1929; October 12, 1929; February 3, 1930; September 23, 1931, page 3; and September 30, 1962); R. Bruce Stephenson, *Visions of Eden*; W.L. Straub, *History of Pinellas County Florida*; and communication with William C. Ballard.

Birth of Our County

The Pinellas Peninsula had been part of Hillsborough County from its beginning in 1834. According to historian Karl H. Grismer, Hillsborough County commissioners had a long history of neglecting the Pinellas Peninsula. Little was spent on roads and bridges, and money appropriated for schools was inadequate. This did not set well with the people living in Pinellas. In 1906, J.W. Williamson of Clearwater announced his plans to present a "county separation" proposal at the next session of the state legislature. On February 20, 1907, the boards of trade of St. Petersburg, Clearwater and Tarpon Springs formed the County Division Organization to petition the legislature for a new county. Those advocating for splitting off from Hillsborough County and forming a new Pinellas County were referred to as "divisionists." *St. Petersburg Times* editor William L. Straub immediately took up the cause and began to wage a campaign for the proposal throughout the spring and summer of 1906: "The little end of a big county like Hillsborough will never get anything like its due until it levies, collects and expends its own taxes."

On February 23, 1907, Straub wrote a lengthy editorial entitled "Pinellas County," later known as the "Pinellas County Declaration of Independence." He argued that division from Hillsborough was warranted by geography, demography and economics. Specifically, he noted that it could take as much as two days to transact business at the county seat in Tampa because of its great distance from St. Petersburg. Travel by auto in the early 1900s from St. Petersburg to Tampa was impossible over roads that were nothing more than trails. Travel by train required a full day's ride with two stops on the way. Boat travel was faster, but schedules were such that it was not always possible to return the same day. Straub added that while physical distance was a major problem in itself, there was also the problem of county government responding first to those closest to it—and to those with the most votes. "Pinellas Peninsula is so entirely and everlastingly cut off from the rest of Hillsborough County that it is and would be entirely and everlastingly—physically impossible—for its people to receive anything like a reasonable or fair share of the common benefits of government. The laws of nature and of human nature prohibit it," Straub added.

Straub also noted that Pinellas's population was more than that in fifteen other counties and that thirteen counties were operating on less revenue than Pinellas was paying in taxes to Hillsborough. Were this revenue going to Pinellas, it would have "the best system of roads in Florida." Of particular interest to a newspaper owner and editor, he also noted that the *Tampa Times* received 50 percent of all county printing revenue, while all Pinellas printers combined received less than 1 percent.

While Straub's editorializing would later get quite heated, at this point it was still temperate. He wrote, "The writer intends no criticism of Tampa and its people here. All good citizens of the West Coast [the Pinellas Peninsula] are proud of Tampa as one of the South's great cities."

The boards of trade proposal and Straub's editorial triggered a storm of protest in Tampa. The *Tampa Times* judged the separation proposal to be "obnoxious from all standpoints" and asked, "What child was ever benefited from being taken from the breast of the nourishing mother?" The Tampa Board of Trade, led by attorney Peter O. Knight, joined in opposition. It mustered forces on both sides of the bay. In Pinellas, there was concern that political independence would be followed by a substantial tax increase. There was also concern in Upper Pinellas, partly promoted by anti-division Tampa interests, that St. Petersburg would dominate a new county. To counter this concern, Straub suggested that Clearwater should be the site of the new county seat and that a majority of the five commissioners come from Upper Pinellas. This suggestion was unpopular in St. Petersburg, but Straub managed to garner the necessary support.

County division petitions were circulated in March 1907, and Straub drafted a county division bill presented to the legislature in April. On May 3, the bill reached the House floor, where it was first passed by a vote of twenty-eight to twenty-one. However, it was blocked in the Senate by Hillsborough's Senator J.E. Crane. This caused uproar in Pinellas, as Crane had earlier promised not to block the measure. He claimed that he did so after discovering that the measure passed the House as the result of bribery, a charge that was unfounded. Straub's reaction to Crane's action was manic. He wrote a front-page parody of the event in which he is kidnapped by a bunch of Tampa pirates, even going so far as to draw a cartoon naming eleven of the "pirates"—all Tampa politicians who opposed division of the county.

Over the next four years, the Pinellas and Hillsborough factions continued to battle. For most of that time, the Hillsborough faction prevailed. But in 1911, the Pinellas faction finally succeeded after a bitter struggle. In the final battle, the political climate became especially ugly. As historian Ray Arsenault wrote, the Hillsborough faction even charged that "Straub and his associates were radical Yankee socialists who had no respect for Southern traditions. As one renegade St. Petersburg resident who testified on behalf of the Tampans told a legislative committee: 'Leave us to be controlled by Tampa…; it is at least a southern city, dominated by southern men, southern traditions, southern ideals and sympathies.'" Historian Karl Grismer wrote that "Tampa newspapers published vitriolic editorials by the score, denouncing Pinellas and everyone in it. St. Petersburg newspapers retaliated with more editorials which almost burned the paper on which they were printed."

The Tampa papers referred to the divisionists as "vandals," and Straub was the "head devil" among them. They also accused Straub of wanting to create a new county controlled by a "combination of Republicans and socialists." Others added blacks and trade unionists to the list. Straub, in turn, spoke of Tampa "interests" as having an "attitude of arrogance, selfishness, injustice and coercion to the end…They seem to appreciate no other policy in political affairs, and remain blind to the fact that that has already given their great and splendid city the most unsavory reputation of any city in Florida."

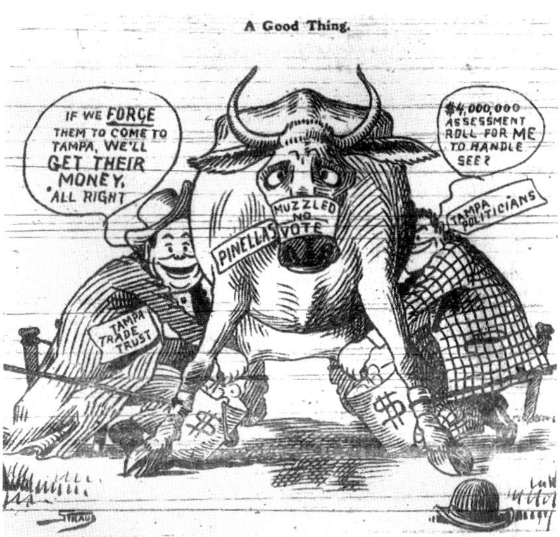

"A Good Thing!" Hillsborough exploiting the Pinellas Peninsula. William L. Straub cartoon, *St. Petersburg Times.*

During the year previous to the 1911 session, Straub sent subscriptions to his paper to every member of the legislature with the intent of persuading them to vote for Pinellas independence. Throughout the year, the newspaper ran numerous articles and cartoons on why Pinellas deserved to be separated from Hillsborough. As this was something the Tampa papers did not do, the effort paid off.

However, there was one more challenge by the anti-division forces in Tampa. During the 1910 state elections, they managed to replace the pro-division state legislator, John S. Taylor, representing the Pinellas section of Hillsborough County, with an anti-division candidate. Straub gave Taylor high praise in his history of Pinellas County for his contributions to formation of the county, perhaps somewhat generously calling him the "Father of Pinellas County." Another key division leader praised by Straub was S.D. Harris, a St. Petersburg undertaker, school board member and activist who later became a successful politician and juvenile judge. But despite Taylor's defeat, the divisionists continued to press their case.

The Pinellas Separation Bill (#247) passed the House on May 5 by a vote of 28 to 18, ironically over the objection of the newly elected legislator from Pinellas. It passed the Senate by a vote of 20 to 9, with the support of Hillsborough senator Don C. McMullen on May 18. The bill was signed into law by Governor Albert W. Gilchrist on May 23. It called for a popular referendum requiring a three-fifths vote for the new county to be finally approved. In an effort to stave off approval, Hillsborough built a new bridge between Seminole and the beaches. A month before the election, the bridge collapsed when a team of mules hauling lumber tried to cross it. Needless to say, Straub made the most of this as an example of Hillsborough incompetence. On November 14, the peninsula's voters approved the creation of the new county by a vote of 1,379 to 505. St. Petersburg voted for it overwhelmingly (232 to 37) as did Clearwater (232 to 37). But some Upper Pinellas areas voted against it, notably Tarpon Springs (44 to 204) and Dunedin (22 to 56). The streets of St. Petersburg and Clearwater were filled by persons celebrating the victory.

The first commissioners were to be appointed by the governor, and according to Arsenault, a local committee had sent a proposed slate giving the upper county three of the five seats. The idea of a slate became controversial, and the divisionists proposed to the governor that there be a primary election. The governor agreed. The election, in which only white males could participate, was held on December 7. The first commissioners were Frank A. Wood and Oliver T. Railsback of St. Petersburg, Soloman Smith Coachman of

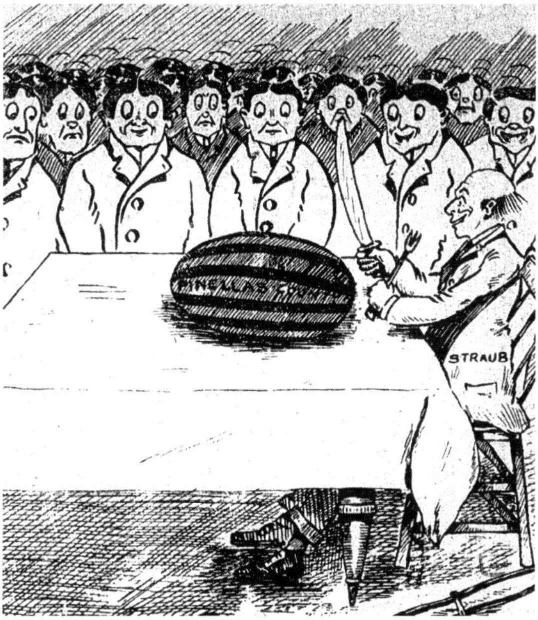

Tarpon Springs Leader cartoon depicting Straub carving up the spoils after Pinellas gained its independence. Straub had the integrity to publish the cartoon on the front page of his *St. Petersburg Times*.

Clearwater, Levin D. Vinson of Tarpon Springs and Jefferson T. Lowe of Anona. The county became a new legal entity on January 1, 1912 (a legal challenge to the division law was denied by the Florida Supreme Court on December 8); 2012 is the centennial year.

But that did not end the story. During the fight for independence, Straub had obtained Upper Peninsula's support by working out a compromise that not only made Clearwater the county seat but also gave Upper Pinellas three of the county's five commissioners. While most of St. Petersburg's leaders supported this arrangement, there was one notable exception: Noel Mitchell. Mitchell was a leading real estate broker known as the "Sand Man" (he works so hard for you he never sleeps) and later was city mayor.

Mitchell offered the new county an entire block in St. Petersburg if it would be used as the new county seat. Clearwater advocates countered by working day and night to construct a makeshift up-county courthouse. State law at the time provided that once a courthouse had been built, a new election to change the county seat could not be held for twenty years. But nothing was to be taken for granted. There were rumors that the new makeshift courthouse would be burned by interests from South County. Guards were posted to prevent this from happening. As Arsenault wrote, "In the end, the courthouse survived, and Clearwater became a permanent county seat. But hard feelings engendered by the county seat controversy would linger for decades."

Despite Straub's designation of John S. Taylor as the "Father of Pinellas County," the title really belongs to Straub himself. While many helped to make Pinellas independent, Straub played the leading role. As Grismer wrote, the establishment of Pinellas County "was advocated and led from the beginning by W.L. Straub…and the victory that was finally won was due largely to his perseverance." At the same time Straub was advocating for an independent Pinellas, he was also advocating for preservation of the St. Petersburg downtown waterfront for parkland and recreational use. In the case of the waterfront, he achieved his goal by finding a win-win solution in supporting a commercial port to the south of the proposed park at Bayboro. He also found a win-win solution to bring about the creation of Pinellas County by supporting location of the county seat at Clearwater and allocation of three of the first five commissioners to the upper county.

The story of Pinellas's birth is a long and complicated one, with a vast number of resource materials, and it is deserving of a serious book in itself.

Resources used in this chapter include Raymond Arsenault, *St. Petersburg and the Florida Dream: 1888–1950*; Rick Baker, *Mangroves to Major League*; *Evening Independent* (especially November 17, 1911, page 1; November 20, 1911, page 4); Walter P. Fuller, *St. Petersburg and Its People* (see page 129 regarding Straub's compromise); Sue Search Goldman, *History of the Board of County Commissioners of Pinellas County*; Karl H. Grismer, *The Story of St. Petersburg* and *The History of St. Petersburg*; Will Michaels, "Birth of Our County: Centennial Year," *Northeast Journal*, 2011; Pinellas County Planning Department, *Pinellas County Historical Background*; Milton O. Polk, "William L. Straub and the Birth of Pinellas County," *St. Petersburg Times*, January 22, 1989, page 4D; *St. Petersburg Times* (especially June 8, 1907; June 22, 1907, pages 1 and 4; June 28, 1907, page 4; June 28, 1907, page 4; April 7, 1911, pages 1 and 3; April 18, 1911, page 1; April 21, 1911, page 1; May 19, 1911, page 1; May 23, 1911, pages 1–2; May 30, 1911, page 1; June 2, 1911, page 1; June 8, 1911, page 1; September 19, 1911, page 1 for Seminole Bridge; November 17, 1911, page 1 for primary election); William L. Straub, *History of Pinellas County, Florida*; and communication with Neil C. McMullen, grandson of Senator Don C. McMullen.

World's First Airline

Each year, the Tony Jannus Distinguished Aviation Society celebrates the world's first airline and its record-breaking pilot, Tony Jannus. And where was this airline? New York? Chicago? London? Berlin? No. The world's first airline originated in St. Petersburg, Florida.

The year 1914 was a benchmark year in our city. Two events occurred that year that would affect our history for years to come. One was the beginning of St. Petersburg's Major League Baseball spring training tradition (discussed in later chapters), and the other was the launching of the world's first airline.

The world's first regularly scheduled heavier-than-air airline took off from the Municipal Pier in St. Petersburg on New Year's Day 1914. The airline was known as the St. Petersburg–Tampa Airboat Line. It was organized just a few months before that New Year's first takeoff. The airline was the brainchild of Percival E. Fansler, a Jacksonville-based electrical engineer. Fansler enlisted the support of Thomas Benoist (pronounced ben-*wah*), an early airplane manufacturer who arranged for the planes—or, more precisely, the airboats. The craft was known as Benoist Airboat Model XIV, no. 43 (or *Benoist*). The model number referred to the year in which the plane was to be offered for sale (1914). The number indicated that it was the forty-third aircraft to be built from initiation of the Benoist Aeroplane Company. The Benoist Airboat was an early version of what we now know as a seaplane, able to take off and land on water. This was a necessity at the time as St. Petersburg had plenty of water but no airports. Our first airport,

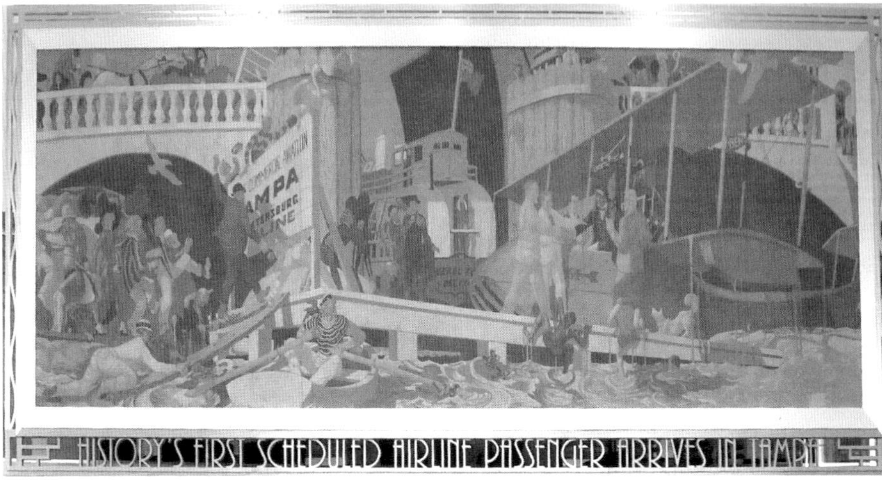

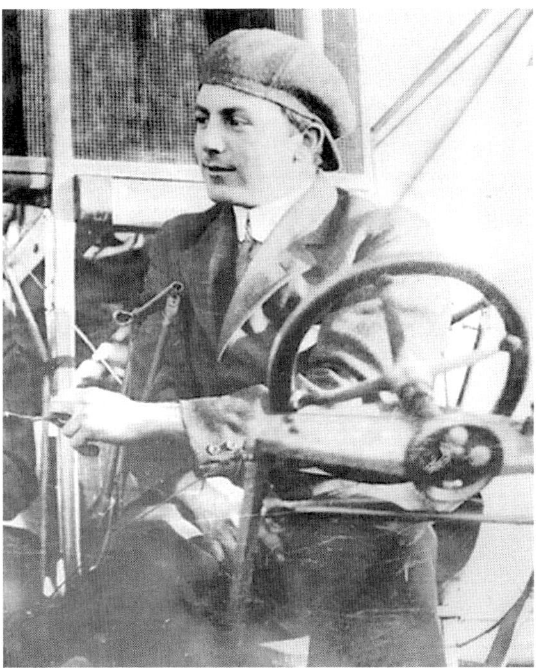

Top: Mural by Works Progress Administration (WPA) artist George Snow Hill at Tampa International Airport. The mural depicts the landing of the first flight of the world's first airline in Tampa. The mural reverses the name of the airline from "St. Petersburg–Tampa Airboat Line" to "Tampa–St. Petersburg Airboat Line." *Courtesy Ann Steele.*

Left: Tony Jannus at College Park, Maryland, 1911. Jannus attended public school in Washington, D.C., and worked as a mechanic after graduating. His work repairing engines led to his career in aviation. *Courtesy St. Petersburg Museum of History.*

Piper-Fuller Airport in the Jungle area of west St. Petersburg, did not open until 1926. Airboat no. 43 was supplemented a little later by a second airboat, no. 45. The two airboats made up the airline's total fleet. No. 43 accommodated one passenger in addition to the pilot. No. 45 was somewhat larger and capable of accommodating two. Benoist also provided the pilot,

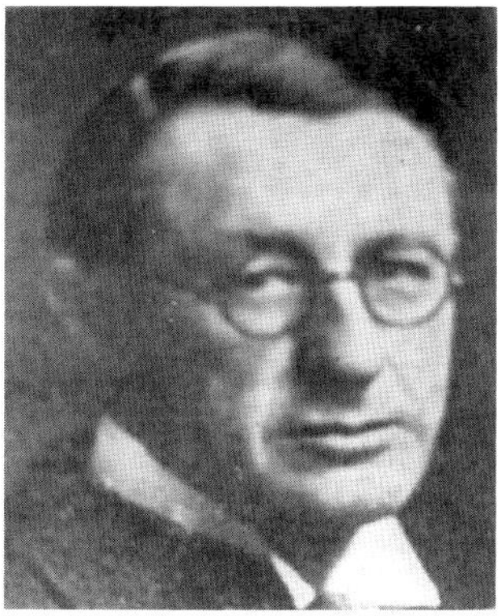

Mayor Noel Mitchell, here in 1920, was a leader in bringing new ideas to St. Petersburg, including green benches, aviation and tent cities for tourists. *Courtesy St. Petersburg Museum of History.*

Antony Habersack Jannus. "Tony" Jannus was a test pilot for Benoist who set early records for passenger flight time and for overwater flight in 1913, and he was the pilot when Albert Berry made the first successful parachute jump. He also held the first federal airline license.

But this world first would never have been possible without the backing of Board of Trade manager L.A. Whitney and businessman and later city mayor Noel Mitchell. In order to make his plan for a new airline work, Fansler needed the support of the St. Petersburg business community and the city's government. He also needed a subsidy to help reduce the financial risk to Tom Benoist. Fansler made his proposal to Whitney, who immediately pledged $1,200 to subsidize the airline. Whitney then referred Fansler to Mitchell, who pledged another $1,000. Mitchell then gathered eleven other local investors to pledge $100 each to start the airline. The group included Lew Brown, publisher of the *Evening Independent*; C. Perry Snell; George Gandy; and Charles Roser. Mitchell even got the city to build a hangar for the airboat on the north side of the approach to the Municipal Pier, at the foot of Second Avenue Northeast.

"Tony Jannus Will Make First Flight Thursday," read the headline of the *St. Petersburg Daily Times* on December 30, 1913. On January 1, three thousand people gathered to see the first flight of this fledgling airline. This was a huge crowd for the city considering that the permanent population was perhaps seven thousand people at the time. Among the crowd was the humorist Will Rogers, who was performing at the Johnny Jones Circus in St. Petersburg. In a charity auction to raffle off the first flight ticket, former St. Petersburg mayor Abe Pheil had bid $400 for the privilege of being the first passenger. Invited to say a few words just prior to takeoff, Percy Fansler commented, "The Airboat Line to Tampa will be only a forerunner of great activity along these lines in the near future…what was impossible yesterday is an accomplishment of today—while tomorrow heralds the unbelievable."

Jannus then took off, skimming across the bay at a height of fifty feet. After a twenty-three-minute flight, including a stop to adjust the drive shaft, Jannus and his single passenger, Abe Pheil, touched down on the Hillsborough River in Tampa. An even larger crowd of 3,500 greeted the

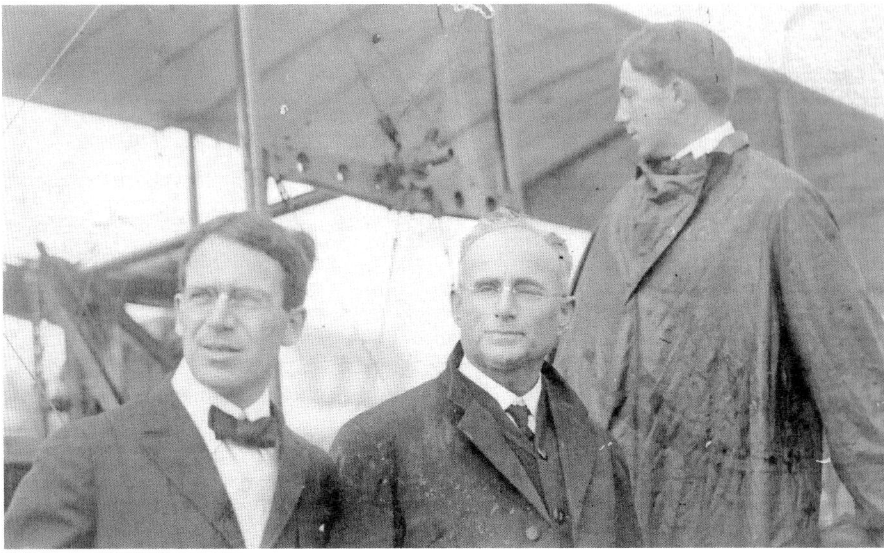

Percy Fansler (left), former St. Petersburg mayor Abe Pheil (center) and Tony Jannus pose in front of the St. Petersburg–Tampa Airboat Line's Benoist Airboat, 1914. *Courtesy St. Petersburg Museum of History.*

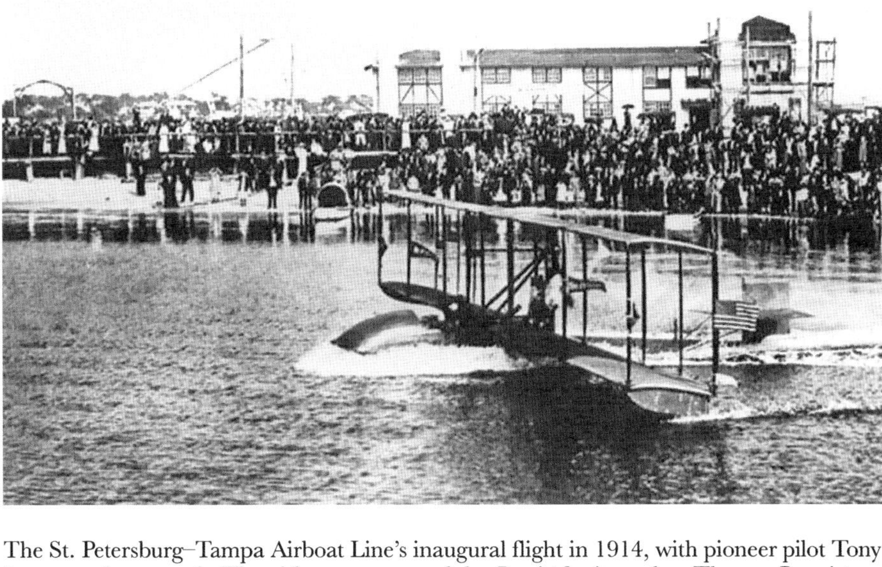

The St. Petersburg–Tampa Airboat Line's inaugural flight in 1914, with pioneer pilot Tony Jannus at the controls. The airboat was named the *Benoist* for its maker, Thomas Benoist. *Courtesy St. Petersburg Museum of History.*

Benoist in Tampa. Tampa mayor Donald B. McKay welcomed Jannus and Pheil after a short delay. The return trip took only twenty minutes, given the benefit of a favorable wind and no stop on the bay.

Mayor Pheil was a major figure in St. Petersburg's early history. Pheil owned the St. Petersburg Novelty Works, which was a building supply and sawmill business. He did much to improve downtown street conditions and was instrumental in bringing manufactured gas to the city. He served as mayor from 1912 to 1913. Betsy Pheil, Abe's granddaughter, remembered from family lore that Mayor Pheil tried to keep his sojourn on the world's first flight a secret from her grandmother. How long this lasted is unknown. Probably not long.

Upon arrival back in St. Petersburg, Jannus dropped his flight goggles, breaking the glass. Ten-year-old Judy Bryan ducked under the rope holding back the crowd. Running up to Jannus, she asked if she could have the goggles. Without hesitation, he gave them to her. Then he removed one of the brightly lettered Benoist pennants from the wing and handed that to her also.

In the weeks that followed, Jannus made at least two regularly scheduled round trips a day between St. Petersburg and Tampa, carrying everything from Swift hams to bundles of the *St. Petersburg Daily Times* (the newspaper's name was later shortened to the *St. Petersburg Times*). Cost of a passenger ticket was $5 each way and $5 for each one hundred pounds of freight. This was not cheap, as $5 in 1914, adjusted for inflation, is valued at $115 in 2012. While $5 per trip was high compared with the cost of rail or steamship, it barely covered the cost of operations. When Tom Benoist was asked how he could cover his costs and make a profit, he stated, "There are at present about 30,000 tourists in the area and I believe a great many of them will patronize the airboat line to save time. Besides, I am anxious to demonstrate the capability and practicality of aerial transportation at a price anyone can afford even if such a low rate means a revenue loss to me, for today's loss could very well be tomorrow's profit."

Jannus and the airboat line were also sought after by other local boosters. One of these was George Lizotte, who operated the Bonhomie and later Lizotte Hotels at Pass-a-Grille, now part of St. Pete Beach. Lizotte hired Jannus to fly passengers from Pass-a-Grille. This was another first—the first time an airline had been chartered for commercial purposes. Jannus made forty-two takeoffs at Pass-a-Grille and racked up a total flying time of ten hours and thirty minutes. For this, Lizotte paid Jannus $150. One of these Pass-a-Grille passengers described Jannus's flights, saying, "He never went higher than 500 feet. You rode in an open cockpit, didn't even have

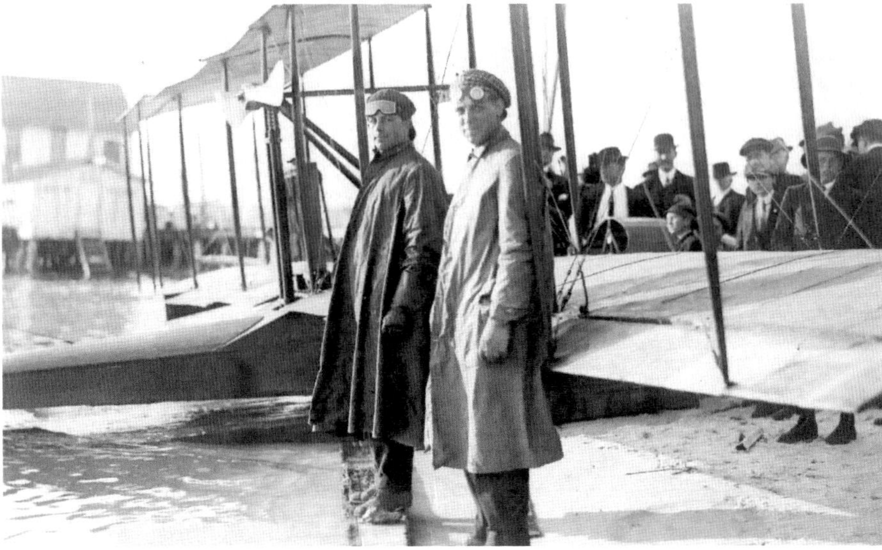

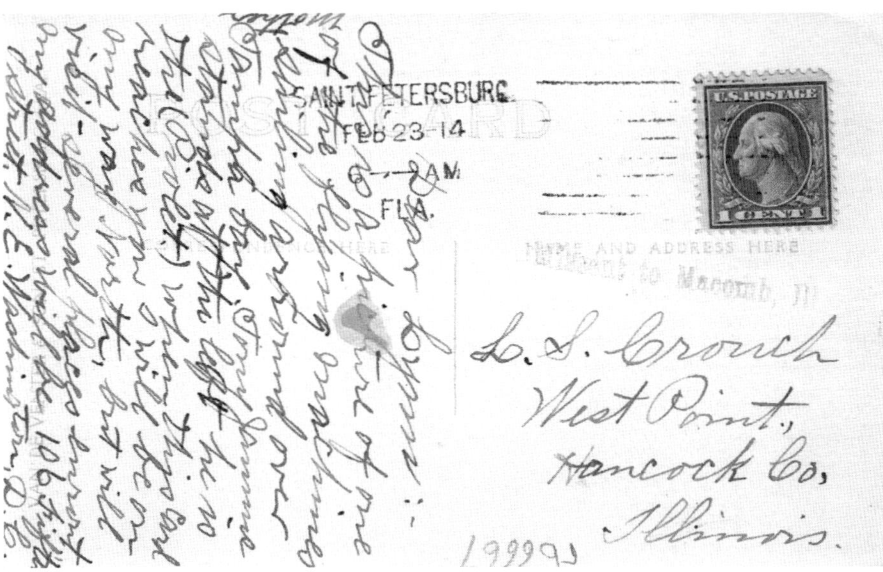

Rare real photo postcard (back and front) showing Tony Jannus (left) and his brother, Roger Weightman Jannus, also a pilot. The message side of this card reads, "This is a picture of one of the flying machines swirling around over Tampa bay. Tony Jannus stands at the left he is the (Piolet)." Ven de Venter & Son, St. Petersburg, 1914. *Courtesy Michaels Family Collection.*

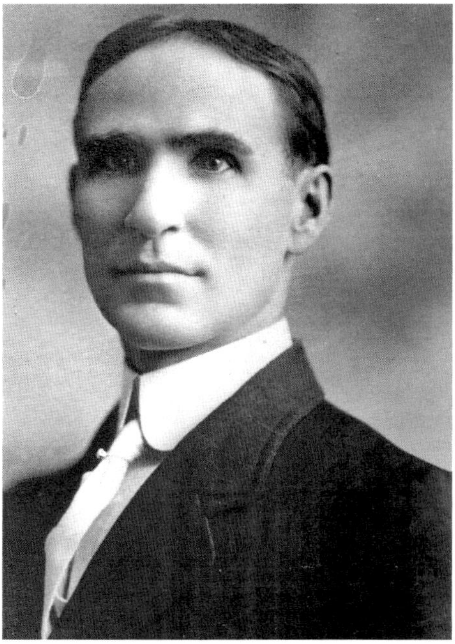

Portrait photo of Thomas Benoist, manufacturer of the Benoist Airboat and a principal in the world's first airline. He built his planes for civilian use, sacrificing some of the speed and maneuverability of other manufacturers that built for military use. Date unknown. *Courtesy City of St. Petersburg.*

a windshield. You wore goggles—we went about 60 miles an hour...The [Boca Ciega] bay was alive with wild ducks. Once Tony reached down and tried to grab one of them as we went through a flock."

Jannus lauded his time in St. Petersburg. In April 1914, he wrote in *Aero and Hydro* magazine, "All told we believe that our work has stamped St. Petersburg as the aviation headquarters of Florida and this is largely due to the hearty cooperation of the city and citizens of the town. There are now hangars that will hold four large [flying] machines and plenty of room to put more and I must say that Tampa Bay is a fine place to fly in winter."

Finally, as the tourist season wore down, the airline suspended its daily operations on March 31. The airline continued for another month with a reduced schedule and flights upon request. The last flight was on May 5. By the end of March, the airline had carried 1,205 passengers and thousands of pounds of freight without a single accident. By comparison, National Airlines, which also began in St. Petersburg in 1934, only carried 400 passengers during its first twelve months of operation. The airline did not break even but came close to it. It appears to have been self-sustaining in two of its three months of operation. In January, it only flew eighteen days. The amount of subsidy drawn from the business community ranged between $540 and $1,740. The exact

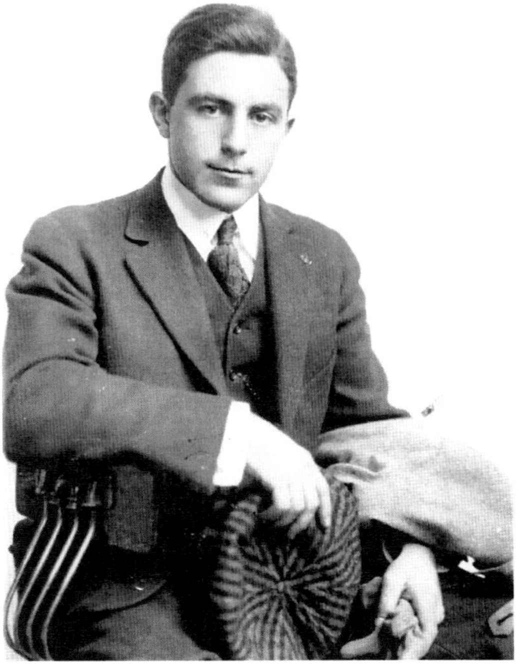

Portrait photo of Tony Jannus inscribed to J.D. Smith "the infallible." Smith was Jannus's mechanic for many years. He was a resident of St. Petersburg beginning a few years after the closing of the St. Petersburg–Tampa Airboat Line, image circa 1914. *Courtesy City of St. Petersburg.*

financial net of its operations is unclear. Given more time for marketing and optimizing operational efficiency, the airline may very well have turned a profit.

Percy Fansler had great hopes for continuing the airline out of St. Petersburg on a permanent basis. He actually bought property on St. Petersburg's Pinellas Point expecting to make St. Petersburg his permanent home. He tried to get the Board of Trade to support reopening the airline. In November 1914, Tony Jannus himself joined with Fansler and others to try to restart the airline, but they were turned down. City business leaders were now giving priority to improving rail service over further investment in the airline. The beginning of World War I may have also been a consideration for not trying further, although the United States would not enter the war for another three years.

The *Benoist* no. 43, also known as the *Lark of Duluth*, was actually owned by banker Julius Barnes of Duluth, Minnesota. He had either loaned or sold it back to the Benoist Company for use in the St. Petersburg–Tampa Airboat Line. After the airline closed, no. 43 was taken by Roger Jannus to San Diego, where it crashed in the ocean in February 1915. L.E. McLain, Benjamin Mack and Byrd Latham from St. Petersburg bought Benoist Airboat no. 45 and took it to Conneaut Lake, Pennsylvania. The plane crashed but was rebuilt and named the *Florida*. The *Florida* was brought back to St. Petersburg, and Tony Jannus returned to fly it. On February 25, 1915, the flying boat crashed in the bay after a wing broke. It was again rebuilt. In November 1916, no. 45 was placed in storage in St. Petersburg, and after that it was lost to history.

Tony Jannus was killed in World War I in an accident while training Russian pilots over the Black Sea for the Curtiss Aeroplane Company. His brother, Roger Jannus, enlisted in the Aviation Branch of the United States Signal Corps during World War I and was killed in 1918 at Issoudon, France, when his de Havilland-4 burst into flames in midair. (The de Havilland was known as the "Flying Coffin.") In referring to Tony Jannus, R.E.G. Davies, curator of air transport at the Smithsonian Institution National Air and Space Museum, said it best, "Of all the early aviators, his career and achievements were possibly the most influential before the outbreak of the First World War. Had Jannus lived, Charles Lindberg would have had a worthy rival."

Jannus's achievements and the significance of the world's first airline have long been recognized. In 1964, the St. Petersburg and Tampa Chambers of Commerce established the Tony Jannus Distinguished Aviation Society to annually honor Jannus and the first airline. The Jannus Society's annual award is known as civil aviation's premier recognition for extraordinary accomplishment. Past recipients include such aviation icons as Donald Douglas, Captain Eddie Rickenbacker, Lieutenant General James H. Doolittle, Frank Borman, Charles Yeager, Sir Freddie Laker and Norman Mineta. Portraits of Jannus and the first airline painted by 1930s Works Progress Administration muralist George Snow Hill hang at Tampa International Airport.

A new wing was built at the St. Petersburg Museum of History in 1992, dedicated to a permanent exhibit featuring the first airline and its founders. This includes a flying reproduction of the *Benoist* no. 43. The goggles and pennant given by Tony Jannus to ten-year-old Judy Bryan, along with a full-size working replica of the Benoist Airboat and other memorabilia relating to the first flight, are on permanent exhibit. Another replica hangs at the St. Petersburg–Clearwater International Airport. In 2006, Tony Jannus's portrait was added to the First Flight Shrine at the Wright Brothers National Memorial in Kitty Hawk, North Carolina. He was designated "A Great Floridian" by the State of Florida in 2010. Downtown's Jannus Landing entertainment center is named after the famed pilot.

In 2010, the American Institute of Aeronautics and Astronautics (AIAA) designated the Central Yacht Basin in St. Petersburg as a Historic Aerospace Site—the place of the first commercial airline flight. In 2011, astronaut Nicole Stott carried the original Benoist pennant on the thirty-ninth and final flight of space shuttle *Discovery* (STS-133). In 2012, efforts were underway to plan the celebration of the centennial of the first airline in 2014, including petitioning of the U.S. Postal Service for the issuing of a Centennial/Jannus commemorative stamp.

The contributions of Percy Fansler and Thomas Benoist have been overshadowed by Tony Jannus over the years. While Jannus was the chief pilot of the St. Petersburg–Tampa Airboat Line and effectively served as its public face, the company could not have accomplished what it did without Fansler and Benoist. The idea of the airline was Fansler's. It was he who enlisted the sponsorship of the Benoist Company, sold the project to the St. Petersburg business community and city government and served as airline manager. Tom Benoist provided the planes and chief pilot Tony Jannus and agreed to operate the airline on a break-even basis. Percival E. Fansler and Tony Jannus were inducted into the Florida Aviation Hall of Fame in 2003. Thomas Benoist was inducted in 2012.

This is a story of both a Florida and world "first." But it is also the story of a future-oriented community that appreciated the latest in invention and was willing to take a risk to see whether the concept of an airline could be of practical value to a booming Florida city—and further add to that boom. While the airline did not quite make a profit, it paid other dividends. As the *Times* reported shortly after the airline was launched, "St. Petersburg is now coming to be known in a way she was never before heard of by people who otherwise would likely never hear of the city." Commenting on the significance of the airline, Tom Benoist, the builder of the Benoist Airboat, said, "Someday people will be crossing oceans on airliners like they do on steamships today." The airline served as a prototype for the future. Others would build on the St. Petersburg–Tampa Airboat Line's experience to create the multibillion-dollar aviation business that the world enjoys today.

> *To me, flying is not the successful defying of death but the indulgence in the poetry of mechanical motion, a dustless, relatively bumpless, fascinating sensation of speed; and abstraction from things material into an infinite space; and abandon that is more exciting but less irritating than any other form of mechanical propulsion...Florida is a live, wide-awake place for aviators and St. Petersburg is the best town for that purpose.*
>
> —*Tony Jannus, 1914*

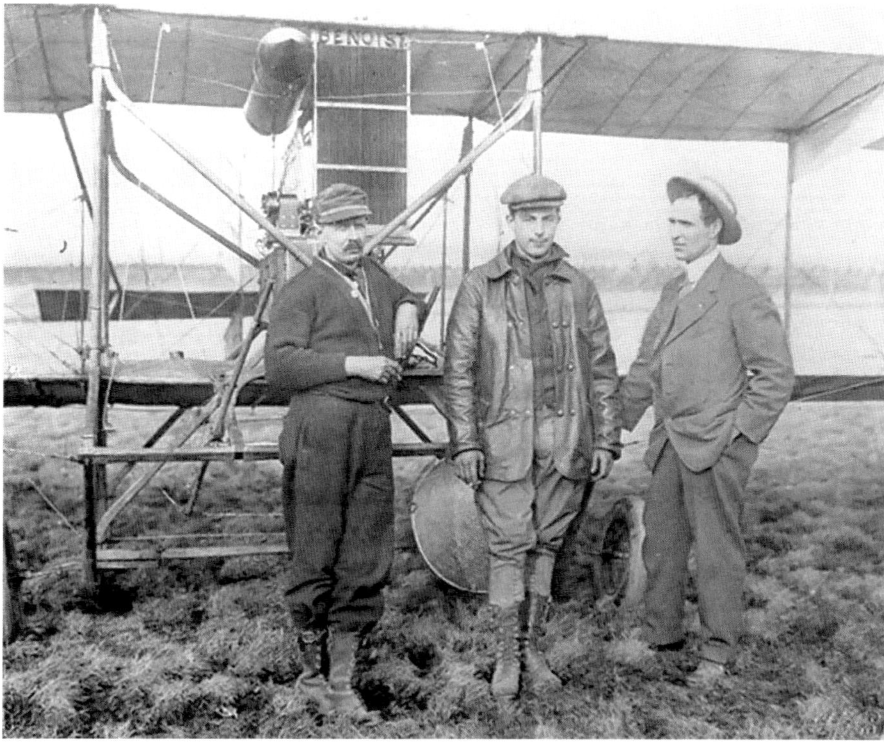

Captain Albert Berry (left), Tony Jannus (center) and Thomas Benoist in front of a Benoist plane at Jefferson Barracks, Missouri, 1912. Tony Jannus was the pilot when Berry made the first successful parachute jump. *Courtesy St. Petersburg Museum of History.*

Resources used in this chapter include Warren J. Brown, *Florida's Aviation History: The First One Hundred Years*; R.E.G. Davies, *Airlines of the United States Since 1914*; Thomas Reilly, *Jannus: An American Flyer*; Florida Aviation Historical Society, *Happy Landings Newsletter* (various); Karl H. Grismer, *The Story of St. Petersburg*; Frank T. Hurley Jr., *Surf, Sand, and Post Card Sunsets: A History of Pass-a-Grille and the Gulf Beaches*; Tony Jannus and Roger Jannus, "Flying Boats and Aeroplanes"; Will Michaels, "Tony Jannus: World's First Airline Pilot Celebrated," *Northeast Journal*, 2006; Gay Blair White, *The World's First Airline*, edited by Warren J. Brown; communication from F. Robert van der Linden, supervisory curator, aeronautics, National Air and Space Museum, to Will Michaels, June 6, 2026; and interview with Betsy Pheil, granddaughter of Mayor Abe Pheil.

St. Petersburg's Passion

Baseball!

The year 1914 was filled with remarkable events in St. Petersburg. That year saw the launching of the world's first airline from the pier on New Year's Day. It was also the year that brought Major League Baseball to St. Pete. Organized amateur baseball had been popular in St. Pete since the formation of the St. Petersburg Saints in 1902, but professional baseball players rarely visited the city before 1910. In 1908, the Cincinnati Reds came to the city to play a single exhibition game against the hometown Saints. In was about this time that city leaders got the idea that the city's most plentiful commodity, sunshine, could be pitched to attract professional baseball to St. Pete and increase tourist dollars as well. In 1912, the Board of Trade tried to get Miller Huggins's St. Louis Cardinals to hold spring training in the city. This effort failed, but later a local group called the St. Petersburg Major League and Amusement Company—there was no need to spell out Major League *Baseball* in the name—was formed under the leadership of Al Lang.

Al Lang arrived in St. Pete in 1910 and six years later became mayor. He was a tidy mayor. One of his first acts was to have "Sign Pulling Down Day." Over St. Pete's early years, commercial signs of all sorts, shapes and sizes proliferated. Lang said they gave the city a "hick look." He also had an ordinance passed requiring the proliferation of Noel Mitchell's multicolored benches to be painted green and built the same size. He did much to improve the infrastructure of the city, paving sandy streets with bricks, constructing seawalls, building a band shell and facilitating construction of the famous open-air post office at First Avenue North and Fourth Street. His efforts

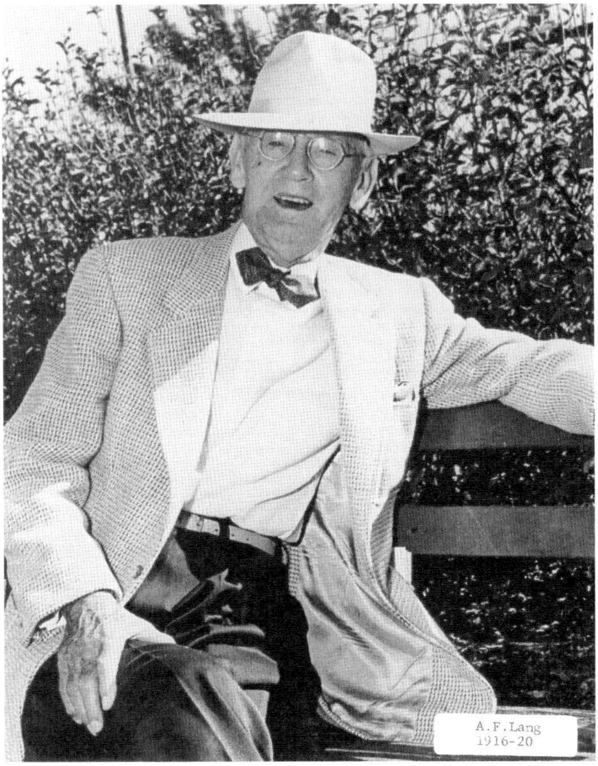

Mayor Al Lang brought Major League Baseball spring training to St. Petersburg, image circa 1950. *Courtesy St. Petersburg Museum of History.*

were not limited to the physical appearance of the city. He also initiated the Festival of the States tradition as a way to build community spirit and foster tourism. But his greatest accomplishment was to bring Major League Baseball to the city.

Lang and the Amusement Company commenced their search for a team. Tampa had landed the National League Chicago Cubs, so St. Petersburg focused on the American League. They sent representatives to each American League team in their attempt to get one to agree to come to St. Pete for spring training. Al Lang first tried to get his favorite team, the Pittsburgh Pirates, but was turned down by owner Barney Dreyfuss, who wrote to Lang, saying, "[Y]ou must think I'm a damn fool, suggesting I train in a little one-tank town that's not even a dot on the map." Finally, the American League's St. Louis Browns (later to become the Baltimore Orioles) agreed to give the city a try.

In early 1914, the Browns and their manager, Branch Rickey, trained at a makeshift ballpark named Sunshine Park. It was located near Coffee Pot

Bayou at the end of Twenty-second Avenue North. A 2,500-seat grandstand was built. Rickey called St. Petersburg "the greatest place in the world." The first game between two major league teams was played in St. Petersburg between the Browns and the Chicago Cubs, with the Cubs winning 3–2. Box seats cost one dollar, grandstand seats fifty cents and bleachers twenty-five cents. The mayor declared a half-day holiday for the event. Schools closed and businesses locked up so everyone could attend. Four thousand "rabid and half-rabid" fans turned out. Later that season, businesses closed their doors every Monday and Wednesday afternoons to allow employees and encourage customers to go to the games. While bringing the Browns to St. Petersburg was a major tourist triumph, it was not a financial success, and the Browns decided to go elsewhere in 1915.

Next, Al Lang arranged for the Philadelphia Phillies to train in St. Pete starting in 1915. Lang came to the city in 1910 from Pennsylvania, where he was prominent in Pittsburgh baseball circles. After training in St. Petersburg, the Phillies won fourteen of their first fifteen games during the regular season, eventually winning the National League pennant. Some said the reason for the Phillies' success was the good training they received in St. Pete. The Phillies baseball coup also put St. Pete in the national baseball limelight. As historian Arsenault stated, "[B]efore long America's pastime had become St. Petersburg's passion."

For the next seventy years—with a few exceptions—the city was host to one and sometimes two major leagues each spring. The Phillies, superstitious about changing socks and spring training venues while winning, kept coming back to St. Petersburg until 1918. During the three years that the Phillies trained in St. Pete, not a single game or practice was canceled because of bad weather. The Boston Braves were enticed to the city in 1921 by the construction of a new Waterfront Park Stadium, a little north of today's Al Lang Field. Babe Ruth and the New York Yankees arrived in 1925. The Braves remained until 1937 and the Yankees until 1961.

Al Lang became a local hero by bringing the Phillies to the city. He became known as St. Petersburg's "Ambassador to Baseball" and was elected mayor in 1916. In addition to the Browns and Phillies, Lang was also instrumental in bringing the Boston Braves (1922), the New York Yankees (1925) and the St. Louis Cardinals (1938), all to "Spetersburg," as he called the city. At the time, the Yankees had been playing in New Orleans, with all its temptations. Lang told Yankees owner Jake Ruppert that the "minds of the players would be more on baseball and less on wine and women" in the little town of St. Petersburg. Lang was likely thinking particularly about Babe Ruth. The true character of St. Petersburg at that time, at least for Ruth and some other major league players, was probably closer to that described by a visiting newspaper reporter in Lee Irby's novel *7,000 Clams*:

> *When the New York Yankees hold a spring training, you can count on two things: good damn baseball and good damn booze. You file your story by noon and that leaves the rest of the day to make mischief until the wee hours. Last night's destination was some watering hole called the Gangplank where scantily clad maidens paraded their exposed flesh and officious waiters poured snifters of just about every libation known in Christendom.*

In 1947, Al Lang Field, on the site of Waterfront Park at the foot of First Avenue South, was named in Lang's honor. This became the new spring training home for the Yankees and the Cardinals. Casey Stengel said of Al Lang that he "had the betterment of baseball and St. Petersburg on his mind both daytime and nighttime." In St. Petersburg, Lang earned the title of "Mr. Baseball." In the larger world of baseball, he was known as "Mr. St. Petersburg" and "Sunshine Al."

Babe Ruth was baseball's king during the 1920s. He was joined on the Yankees team by such baseball icons as Lou Gehrig and Tony Lazzeri. The fact that the Yankees won the World Series three times in the 1920s added even further reflected glory to St. Pete as their spring training host. The Yankees trained at Crescent Lake Park. During the years the Yankees spent most of their spring training in St. Pete, they won twenty pennants and sixteen World Series. The Yankees were in St. Pete for thirty years. Only the Cardinals stayed longer—an amazing fifty-five years in their case.

More than any other single factor, Ruth, the Yankees and their cohorts gave St. Pete national fame and served as a major force in attracting tourists and seasonal residents. The permanent population of the city tripled between 1920 and 1940, and to some extent, this may be attributed to the attraction of world-class baseball. As Mayor Lang reflected, "The Yankees with Babe Ruth and their stars meant millions to this town." In the early 1930s, the Yankees signed a three-year contract to stay at the Don CeSar, which probably saved the hotel from financial ruin. The Yankees and their entourage filled 125 rooms at the Don, although Ruth and Gehrig had penthouses at the Flori-de-Leon at 130 Fourth Avenue North. While the Babe left the Yankees in 1934, the team continued to sparkle with the likes of Joe DiMaggio, Lefty Gomez, Lou Gehrig and Bill Dickey. And then Ruth was back in St. Pete again in 1935 as a member of the Boston Braves.

African Americans created their own baseball teams and leagues. These teams also attracted white spectators, who sat in segregated bleachers. None of this had much effect on the segregation of the time, but as Arsenault stated, "[I]t took some of the sting out of Jim Crow." ("Jim Crow" was the term used for segregationist laws passed around the turn of the last century. It originated from a song-and-dance routine performed by white actors in blackface called "Jump Jim Crow.") In 1938, the St. Louis Cardinals came to St. Pete.

It was the same Branch Rickey who managed the Browns' spring training in St. Petersburg in 1914 who, thirty-three years later in 1947, broke baseball's racial restriction by signing Jackie Robinson with the Brooklyn Dodgers. In 1950, Sam Jethroe of the Boston Braves was the first African American to break the color line in St. Petersburg. This was despite a city law prohibiting integrated play. It took a long time for the ugly grip of segregation to loosen its hold on baseball and the culture supporting it. Local hotels such as the Soreno refused to accommodate African American players, including such future Hall of Famers as Bob Gibson and Elston Howard and future National League president Bill White.

As the number of African American players slowly increased in the major leagues, baseball venues in the South, including St. Petersburg, were challenged to change their ways. In St. Pete, African Americans players were hosted in private homes, and in African American dental surgeon Robert James Swain's Robert James Hotel and his apartments, until the larger hotels removed their restrictions.

Black baseball player Monte Irvin remembered the dark days of segregation:

> *We complained about discrimination in St. Petersburg the year we trained there. We had to stay at a boarding house with one toilet. White players had individual hotel rooms, individual toilets; they ordered dinner from a full menu card. We ate whatever was shoved before us. They had but one idea—to make the team. We had to worry about our rest, our diet, how to get to the ball park, where to relax after games, which store door to open as we walked down the street.*

In 1960, Cardinal player Bill White and local African American leaders Bessie Wynn, Dr. Robert Swain, Dr. Ralph Wimbish and his wife, C. Bette Wimbish, and others openly protested the segregation encountered by African American Cardinal ball players. In 1961, they forced action by refusing to house African American players any more in black facilities. The Cardinals relocated their team to motels in South St. Pete near the Skyway Bridge where all players, black and white, were housed under the same roof. The Yankees threatened to leave the city if the situation was not corrected. They soon relocated to Fort Lauderdale, which offered new and better facilities. If their decision to relocate was, in fact, due to segregation in St. Pete, it has not been made clear to this day. When they moved, the stated reason was to have a spring training city to themselves. But segregation was likely a consideration.

In addition to the Saints, St. Pete's local teams also included Negro League teams such as the Sunshine Babies, the Braves, the Florida Stars, the Pelicans and the Oliver Allouettes. Two of St. Petersburg's outstanding African American players were James F. Oliver who played in the Negro Leagues in the early 1940s, and his son, Nate, who played for the Los Angeles Dodgers in the 1960s. Historic Oliver Field at Campbell Park is named after James Oliver. The Kids and Kubs softball baseball team was organized by the Three-Quarter Century Club in 1930. It became a symbol of what we now called the "active retiree" and of St. Petersburg as an active retirement community. Men had to be seventy-four years of age and older to play. The team's signature uniforms are white and red with bow ties.

St. Petersburg finally got a major league team of its own in 1995, the Tampa Bay Devil Rays. The first game was played against the Detroit Tigers at Tropicana Field, formerly the ThunderDome, on March 31, 1998. The Tigers won 11–6. As local baseball historian A.M. de Quesada stated, "After nearly a century of baseball history in the area, Tampa Bay finally made it to the big league!" Baseball historian Kevin M. McCarthy wrote that if any city deserved the title of "Baseball City" in Florida, it would surely be St. Petersburg. While Mayor Al Lang was right to note the economic impact of the Yankees and Babe Ruth on St. Petersburg, Mayor Lang himself deserves at least equal praise for having the vision to bring major league spring training to the city.

MAJOR LEAGUE TEAMS IN ST. PETERSBURG

Spring Training

St. Louis Browns	1914
Philadelphia Phillies	1915–1918
Boston Braves	1922–1937

New York Yankees	1925–1942, 1946–1950, 1952–1961
St. Louis Cardinals	1938–1942, 1946–1997
New York Giants	1951
New York Mets	1962–1987
Baltimore Orioles	1993–1995
Tampa Bay (Devil) Rays	1998–2008

Regular Season

Tampa Bay (Devil) Rays	1998—present

Sources used in this chapter include Raymond Arsenault, *St. Petersburg and the Florida Dream, 1888–1950*; Rick Baker, *Mangroves to Major League: A Timeline of St. Petersburg, Florida*; Charles Fountain, *Under the March Sun: The Story of Spring Training*; Karl H. Grismer, *History of St. Petersburg*; Scott Taylor Hartzell, *Voices of America: St. Petersburg*; Kevin M. McCarthy, *Baseball in Florida*; Will Michaels, "St. Petersburg's Passion—Baseball," *Northeast Journal*, 2005; Larry Moffi and Jonathan Kronstadt, *Crossing the Line: Black Major Leaguers: 1947–1959*; and A.M. de Quesada, *Baseball in Tampa Bay*.

History of Our Stadiums

In 1908, the Cincinnati Reds came to play a single exhibition game against the St. Petersburg Saints, our city team. It was played on a ball field on the northeast side of Reservoir Lake, now Mirror Lake. Because of flooding, the Saints moved to a new ball field in 1911, at Eighteenth Avenue South near Fortieth Street. The field was named after their manager, C.C. Symonette.

Coffee Pot Park

The Major League and Amusement Company was composed of local entrepreneurs and capitalized at $10,000. After recruiting the St. Louis Browns in 1913, it proceeded to build a grandstand and pay the hotel and transportation expenses of the team. It also agreed to pay the expenses of five sportswriters to accompany the team and report on not just the Browns but also, more importantly, the wonderful city of St. Petersburg.

Four different sites were considered by the Amusement Company for the ballpark. Ultimately, a site was selected at the head of Coffee Pot Bayou in the vicinity of where Granada Terrace is now located. This site belonged to developer C. Perry Snell, who agreed to lease the land to the baseball company for a period of up to six years without cost. Snell likely believed that locating the stadium there would also enhance the value of his real estate. The company had to pay for the stadium. This deal saved the company $18,000 that would have been charged for the land on the next favored site. A contemporary stated that this allowed the company to "test the money-making qualities of a league in this city without sinking [thousands of dollars] into a baseball ground."

In early 1914, the Browns trained at the new ballpark. It was officially named Sunshine Park, but almost everyone referred to it as Coffee Pot Park, as it was located on the south shore of Coffee Pot Bayou. It had a 2,500-seat grandstand and uncovered bleachers with another 2,500 seats. The Browns' manager, Branch Rickey, called Coffee Pot "one of the best training fields in the country." The Browns decided to go elsewhere in 1915. They were followed by the Phillies, who stayed until 1918. There was then a two-year hiatus due to World War I. In 1921 Al Lang negotiated to get the Boston Braves.

WATERFRONT PARK

The president of the Braves told Lang that they would come if a new ballpark was built. St. Petersburg city officials then urged residents to contribute to the cost of a new ballpark, stating that the spring training publicity alone "is worth many times the cost of the ball field." So, in 1921, the City Park Board made available property a little north of today's Al Lang Stadium on a ninety-nine-year lease. Local boosters paid for the construction of a 2,500-seat stadium on the site. The new ball park was completed in 1922, just a few months after the Great Hurricane, and the Braves began play in March. They remained in the city until 1937 and then were immediately replaced by the Cardinals.

In 1924, Yankees manager and St. Petersburg winter resident Miller Huggins convinced the owner of the Yankees, Colonel Jacob Ruppert, to move the Yankees to the city for spring training. As the Braves were already occupying Waterfront Park, the city built a second spring training facility at Crescent Lake. This made St. Petersburg at that time the only spring training city in the nation with two major league teams. Babe Ruth and the New York Yankees arrived in 1925. The Yankees stayed in the city until 1961.

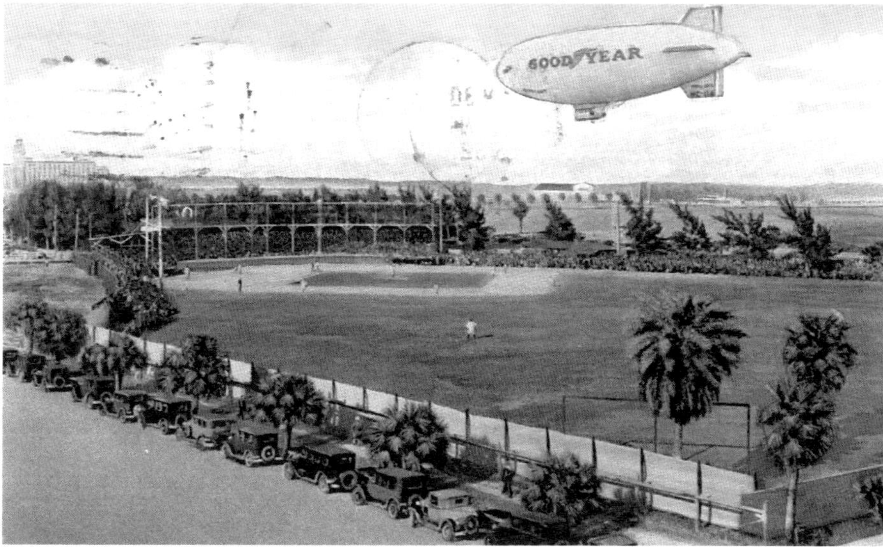

Waterfront Park Field was built in 1921 where today's Progress Energy/Al Lang Stadium ballpark now stands. Al Lang Field replaced Waterfront Park Field in 1947. Blimps were brought to the city in 1929 as tourist attractions and were housed at a city-supported hangar at Albert Whitted Airport. Curt Teich & Company, Chicago. Postcard dated 1932. *Courtesy Michaels Family Collection.*

AL LANG STADIUM

In 1938, the city considered its options regarding a possible new ballpark at Waterfront Park. The old wooden grandstand had insufficient seating capacity and had become a serious fire hazard. Both the Yankees, who played exhibition games there, and the Cardinals objected to building a new facility and urged that improvements be made to the old ballpark. For months, residents debated whether to renovate or to build a new ballpark. Most residents at first sided with the baseball teams, citing financial and aesthetic reasons. It was argued that a new facility would detract from the beauty of the waterfront and lower the value of adjoining real estate. Some environmentalists filed for an injunction against the building of a "nuisance" structure that they said would desecrate the city's waterfront.

At first, the city council proposed to build a steel grandstand that could later be moved to another site. The city council first voted to build a new stadium at Woodland Park near North Kenwood Neighborhood. But in

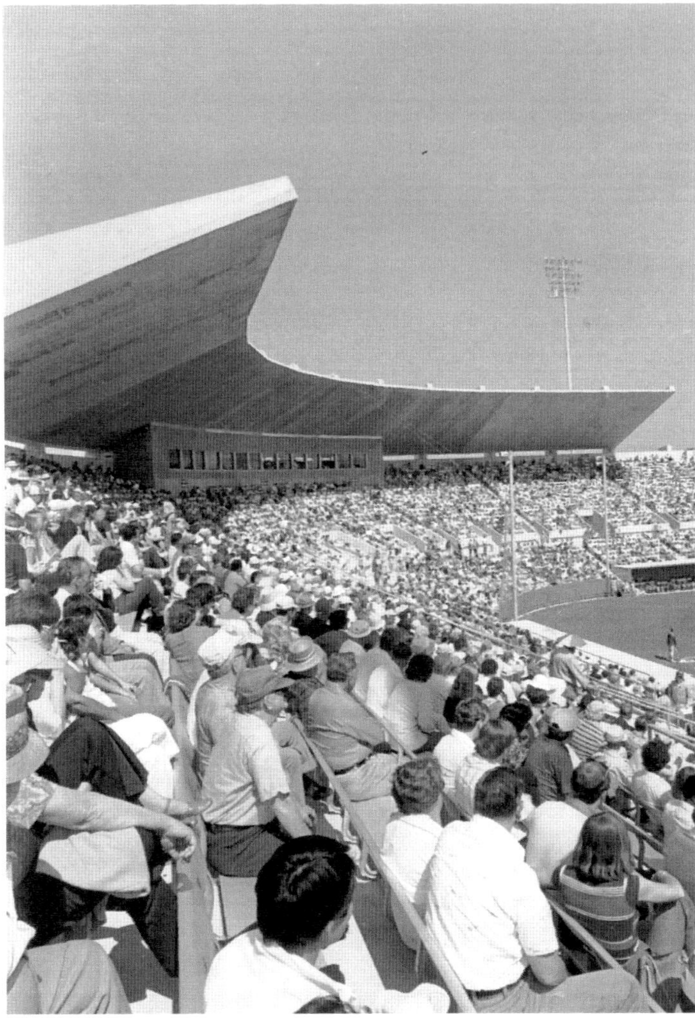

Al Lang Field replaced Waterfront Park Field in 1947. Al Lang Stadium (above) replaced Al Lang Field in 1977. *Photo Courtesy City of St. Petersburg.*

1940, the citizens voted in a referendum three to one in favor of rebuilding on the waterfront. The council then authorized the building of a permanent stadium three hundred feet from the old stadium. Because of the war, construction was delayed. The new Al Lang Field was finally opened in 1947 with 4,300 seats. The first stadium was later demolished, and a new one was built in 1977, financed with a mix of federal and city funds.

TROPICANA FIELD

After the National Football League awarded what became the Tampa Bay Buccaneers to Tampa in 1976, *St. Petersburg Times* publisher Jack Lake began to advocate for a Major League Baseball team in St. Petersburg. For several years, St. Petersburg and Pinellas County baseball boosters sought to get a major league team to come to St. Pete. In 1983, local boosters advocated that the community proceed to build a multipurpose stadium before receiving commitment from a team. In October, the city council voted eight to one to pledge up to $4 million per year to subsidize a stadium. The following month, the county commission followed suit and voted four to three to guarantee construction bonds. One month after that, the city council approved $83 million in bonds.

While St. Petersburg mayor Corinne Freeman was an early supporter of the stadium, she acknowledged building a stadium without the commitment of a team to be "the riskiest gamble" St. Petersburg had ever taken. There was significant opposition among the public, and Mayor Freeman and a city council stadium supporter lost their bids for reelection because of their support for the stadium. It took three more years to overcome the opposition. The building of the stadium was finally approved on a six to three city council vote. No public referendum was required or held. The forty-three-thousand-seat stadium was completed in 1990.

This "build it and they will come" strategy paid off, but not for another five years. After a saga of efforts to engage a major league team—involving the Minnesota Twins, Chicago White Sox, Texas Rangers, Seattle Mariners and San Francisco Giants, as well as the selection of Miami and Denver for new franchises—St. Petersburg was awarded a new franchise in 1995. While the city retained ownership of the stadium, control was given to Vince Naimoli's Tampa Bay Baseball Ownership Group. The team was originally named the Tampa Bay Devil Rays, causing many to think it was located in Tampa rather than St. Petersburg. Use of the manta ray as a team symbol reflected the rich fish life of the St. Petersburg area. The Rays' first game was played in 1998.

Meanwhile, the cost of the stadium had increased from the $85 million approved by the city in 1986 to $138 million by the time the stadium opened in 1990. Renovations needed to prepare it for the 1998 season further pushed the cost to $200 million. The Devil Rays agreed to pay one-third of the increased costs, the county agreed to raise its hotel tax from 3 percent to 4 percent for twenty years to pay its share and the city raised money by selling additional bonds.

The 1.1-million-square-foot stadium was originally named the Florida Suncoast Dome. Later, because the Tampa Bay Lightning hockey team played there, the stadium was renamed the ThunderDome. After securing the Devil Rays, the name was changed to Tropicana Field, after the Tropicana Dole Beverages North America Company, which purchased naming rights for $42 million. In 2004, a team of investors led by Stuart L. Sternberg purchased a controlling interest in the Rays for $65 million. In 2007, the Rays' new owners dropped the "Devil" from their team's name. At the same time, a yellow sunburst was added to the logo, another symbol of the sunshine city.

Also in 2007, the Rays baseball club proposed demolishing Tropicana Field and replacing it with a mixed-use retail and residential development, as well as demolishing Al Lang Stadium and replacing it with a new open-air thirty-four-thousand-seat stadium. After considerable community opposition to building such a large stadium on the downtown waterfront, the proposal was withdrawn. The Rays continue to seek a new stadium on an alternative site. Their current lease with the city expires in 2027.

What lessons can be learned from St. Pete's baseball history? Baseball was brought to St. Petersburg through a series of local government and private investor partnerships. Local government frequently invested public resources to build stadiums and attract and keep major league teams. The cost of building Tropicana Field greatly exceeded the original projection. Significant waterfront land was dedicated to baseball, beginning in 1914. The building of Tropicana Field ten blocks from the waterfront was the first significant departure from this. St. Petersburg's success so far has been either with open-air stadiums used for springtime training, when temperature and humidity are relatively cool, and the air-conditioned Tropicana Stadium. As St. Petersburg's economy has diversified and grown, the relative contribution of baseball, while important, has declined.

Beginning as early as 1938, the building of new stadiums became increasingly controversial, although all were approved until the Rays' 2007 proposal. There is great sensitivity to the possibility of any new building on the downtown Waterfront Parks. Since the park was established in 1909, it has been the third rail of St. Petersburg politics. What does the future hold for baseball and stadiums in St. Petersburg? As Yogi Berra said, "It's difficult to make predictions, especially about the future." In assessing history, one has to examine how the context of events may have changed. But one thing is certain. Baseball, like the Waterfront Parks, has been a big part of St. Petersburg's history and sense of place.

FIELDS AND STADIUMS

Name	**Date**	**Note**
(no name)	1908–1911	North side of Mirror Lake. Used by St. Petersburg Saints.
Symonette Field	1911	Tangerine Avenue (Eighteenth Avenue South, west of Fortieth Street). Used by Saints and named after manager C.C. Symonette.
Coffee Pot Park	1914–19	Also known as Sunshine Park. Head of Coffee Pot Bayou.
Waterfront Park (Field)	1922–47	Also known as St. Petersburg Athletic Park (First Avenue South at the Bay; site of parking lot for present Al Lang Stadium)
Albert F. Lang Field	1947	(Just south of Waterfront Field)
Crescent Lake Baseball Park	1925	Renamed Miller Huggins Field in honor of Yankees manager in 1931; renamed Huggins-Stengel Field in honor of later manager Casey Stengel in 1962.

Name	Date	Note
Northeast Baseball Complex	1955	Cardinals spring training field.
Payson Field	1962	West of Tyrone Square Mall. Spring training field for the Mets. Named after Joan Payson, first Mets owner. Later renamed after Raymond A. Naimoli, former senior vice-president and CFO of Devil Rays.
Al Lang Stadium	1977	Al Lang Field rebuilt and redesignated "Stadium." In 2003, the name was formally changed to Progress Energy Park (home of Al Lang Field).
Florida Suncoast Dome	1990	Opened at a former gas plant site. Renamed the ThunderDome in 1993 and Tropicana Field in 1997.

Sources used in this chapter include Bob Andelman, *Stadium for Rent*; Raymond Arsenault, *St. Petersburg and the Florida Dream, 1888–1950*; Rick Baker, *Mangroves to Major League: A Timeline of St. Petersburg, Florida*; Karl H. Grismer, *History of St. Petersburg*; Scott Taylor Hartzell, *Voices of America: St. Petersburg*; Kevin M. McCarthy, *Baseball in Florida*; Will Michaels, "A Passion for Baseball: History of Our Stadiums," *Northeast Journal*, 2008; Paul Pedersen, *Build It And They Will Come*; A.M. de Quesada, *Baseball in Tampa Bay*; *St. Petersburg Daily Times*; Judy Lowe Wells, *C. Perry Snell: His Place in St. Petersburg, Florida History*; and interview with former mayor Corinne Freeman.

Babe Ruth in St. Petersburg

A Soft Spot for Kids

George Herman "Babe" Ruth was sent by his parents in 1902 at the age of seven to live at Baltimore's St. Mary's Industrial School for Boys. The school was actually an orphanage and residential program for delinquent boys. There he remained for the next thirteen years, and it was there he learned to play baseball. It was also at St. Mary's that Ruth was discovered and directly recruited out of the orphanage by the Baltimore Orioles in 1914 at the age of nineteen. He played with the Orioles for less than a year before being sold to the Boston Red Sox. The Sox, in turn, sold him to the New York Yankees in 1920. Ruth came to St. Pete with the Yankees in 1925, although he participated in spring training with the Sox in nearby Tampa in 1919. He left the Yankees in 1934. Ruth again returned to St. Petersburg in 1935 as a member of the Boston Braves.

Longest Homer

The Red Sox and Ruth had spring training in Tampa in 1919. Ruth may have made his first excursion to St. Pete at that time, but no record of that has been found. During the 1919 spring training season, while playing against the New York Giants in Tampa, Ruth hit a home run. For many years, this was considered Ruth's longest home run and was probably longer than any

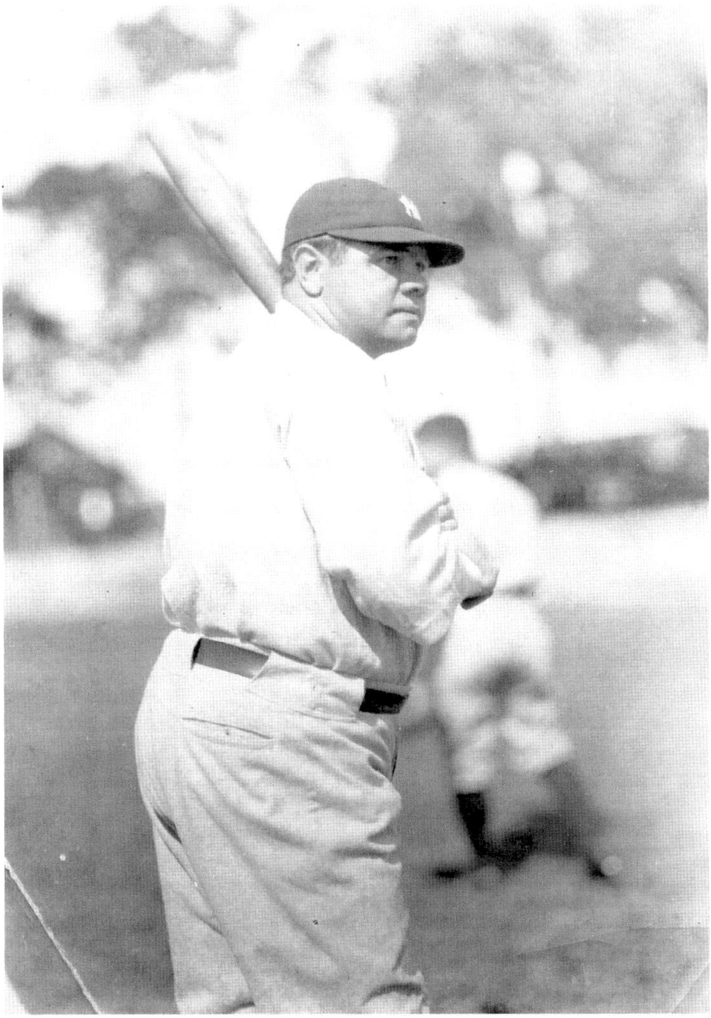

Babe Ruth at Waterfront Park, 1927. *Courtesy St. Petersburg Museum of History.*

other hit by a player during Ruth's time. The feat is commemorated on a plaque at Tampa's Plant Field at the University of Tampa. Baseball historian Leigh Montville wrote that after the game several sportswriters got the Giants right fielder to point out the spot where the ball landed and then measured the distance to home plate. They estimated that Ruth's hit traveled 508 feet in the air and then rolled dead 579 feet from home plate. While the home run's exact distance may be debatable, it was definitely impressive. Giants manager John McGraw stated at the time, "I believe it's the longest hit I ever saw." The ball was subsequently presented to former Chicago Cubs player and evangelist Billy Sunday, who was visiting Tampa at the time. Coincidentally, St. Petersburg mayor Al Lang was in Tampa to lobby the Giants to relocate to St. Petersburg for future spring trainings when Ruth hit his impressive homer. This inspired the mayor to push to get Ruth and the Yankees, rather than the Giants, to come to St. Pete.

It has recently been established that Ruth may have hit an even longer homer in St. Pete during batting practice or a home run exhibition about 1930, though details are unclear. This was a 624.67-foot home run hit from Waterfront Park to the steps of the West Coast Inn across First Street. The ball probably bounced on the way. According to Tim Reid of the St. Petersburg Committee to Commemorate Babe Ruth, this is believed to be the longest hit ever off major league pitching. In 1930, the National League was using a new extra-resilient "rabbit ball," and that may have been a factor. When Ruth was sick with oral cancer and making a last hurrah tour in 1948, he returned to the site of St. Pete's downtown Waterfront Park Stadium. Asked what his greatest accomplishment there was, he replied, "The day I hit the [expletive] ball against that [expletive] hotel!"

Arrival of the Yankees

In 1924, Yankees manager and St. Petersburg winter resident Miller Huggins, along with Mayor Lang, convinced the owner of the New York Yankees, Colonel Jacob Ruppert, to move the Yankees to the city for spring training. As the Boston Braves were already occupying Waterfront Park, the city built a second spring training facility at Crescent Lake. Babe Ruth and the Yankees arrived in 1925.

Every February and March, baseball fans jammed the stands at Crescent Lake Park to catch a glimpse of Ruth. On February 23, 1925, some five thousand fans attended the dedication of the Crescent Lake Baseball Park. On that same day, the New York Yankees held their first spring training workout in St. Pete. The Yankees stayed in St. Pete until 1961, with a couple of interruptions during World War II. During that period, they won twenty pennants and sixteen World Series.

Babe Ruth's first arrival in St. Pete as a player for the Yankees was met with the proverbial brass band. The *New York Times* coverage of the event was titled, "Home-Run King Heads Triumphal March on Arrival at St. Petersburg." The March 1 article went on to note:

> *Weighing very little more than a modest 225 pounds, George Herman Ruth reported to manager Miller Huggins late this afternoon…The earthquake in Northern regions yesterday was a mild little affair compared to the reverberating tremors which shook St. Petersburg when the King of Swat joined the social colony here. The occasion marked the official inauguration of the baseball and social season on the west coast. All the beauty and chivalry of St. Petersburg was on hand to welcome the great Babe, and his progress from the station to the Princess Martha Hotel was nothing less than a triumphal march. Al Lang, the chief baseball mogul of Florida, was at the depot to extend the hand of welcome to Ruth, and with Al were representatives of all the civic and business organizations of the municipality. As Ruth neared the hotel the Scottish Highlander Band of this city broke into "Hail to the Chief." It was a very striking occasion.*

The article went on to report:

> *Ruth said he weighed 225 pounds and he looked even heavier. He admitted that in his month's stay at Hot Springs* [Arkansas] *he has succeeded in ridding himself of only fifteen pounds, but the big fellow seemed anything but worried about his general health. "I'll be down to 215 pounds by the opening of the season," he said. "That will be slightly over my usual weight, but I'm not worrying. Another five pounds won't hurt any. As long as my legs and arms and shoulders are all right and there is nothing wrong with my batting eye, I'll be all right. I don't remember ever feeling better and if I don't lead the league again in batting it won't be the fault of my condition. Anyway, if the American League pitchers walk me as much as they did last year, I won't have to be in condition. Anybody can walk to first base."*

The Yankees trained at Crescent Lake, complete with the occasional alligator crawling out of the lake onto the field. On the Yankees' very first day of training, Ruth had been shagging fly balls for a short time in the outfield, which bordered the lake, when he suddenly returned to the dugout.

Manager Miller Huggins asked him what the problem was. Ruth replied, "I ain't going out there anymore. There're alligators out there." There were also a lot of Ruth's baseballs out there.

The 1926 season saw Ruth arrive in St. Pete a lot trimmer after ending the 1925 season overweight and out of shape. A reporter remarked that he looked like he had found St. Petersburg's famous Fountain of Youth. Upon returning to New York in 1925, Ruth had connected with Art McGovern, a personal trainer for the rich and famous. McGovern's program apparently worked. In 1926, the Crescent Lake ballpark outfield was extended to prevent Ruth from hitting balls into the lake. It didn't work. On a single day in 1928, Babe hit six balls into the lake. No major league player has hit even a single ball into the lake since. Crescent Lake was then 530 feet from home plate at the right field line.

The year 1927 saw Ruth establish his long-standing record of sixty home runs in a single season. While this record has since been surpassed by Roger Maris, Mark McGuire, Sammy Sosa and Barry Bonds, Ruth still holds the record for most home runs in a 154-game season. (Ruth was also playing under more restrictive rules for home runs than are current players.) Ruth's granddaughter, Linda Ruth Tosetti, described Ruth's ability to swivel at bat. "His torque was extreme. In some photos he actually has his back to the pitcher waiting for the pitch." Ruth held his breath when he swung the bat. If he had breathed, he would have generated even more power. He used bats that weighed as much as fifty-four ounces at a time when most players used bats weighing from thirty-six to forty-five ounces. Negro League star and Floridian "Buck" O'Neil said of Ruth's hitting, "I never heard a bat make a sound like that. It was something."

Additionally, Ruth was an accomplished pitcher and outfielder. As a pitcher he scored ninety-four wins and held a World Series record of 29 2/3 consecutive scoreless innings, set in 1918, which was not broken until 1961 by Whitey Ford. As an outfielder, he had astonishing range for his bulk, a powerful arm and keen baseball sense. It was said that he never made a mental error like throwing to the wrong base. At one point in his career Ruth underwent physiological testing at Columbia University. While the results of the testing have since been criticized for being compared with an inappropriate norm group, at the time he was declared "90 per cent efficient" compared with an average of 60 percent.

RUTHAMANIA

Ruth was everywhere in St. Petersburg. He stayed in every major hotel—the Princess Martha, the Vinoy, the Rolyat (Taylor spelled backward), the Sunset, the Dennis and the Jungle Club. In the early 1930s, Ruth and Lou Gehrig leased separate penthouses at the Flori-de-Leon, 130 Fourth Avenue Northeast, while the rest of the team stayed at the Don CeSar at St. Pete Beach. The city was seized with "Ruthamania." Babe Ruth look-alike contests were held. Racing hounds were named after Ruth at the local derby ("Flying Babe Ruth"). Ruth is reported to have bet $1,000 on a race at the derby—perhaps that was the hound he bet on. Real estate brokers exploited his name in the classified ads of the local paper: "Babe Ruth could easily knock a ball from this $2,750 lot."

As a promotion, Rutland Brothers clothing store on one occasion showered the city from the air with Baby Ruth candy bars attached to little parachutes. One of Ruth's favorite haunts was the Gangplank Night Club at the Jungle Prada, where he and many others sipped "Bimini Tea." It is also rumored that Ruth married Claire Hodgson at the Gangplank in a civil ceremony before the church wedding in New York in 1929, but this has never been documented and is unlikely.

While spring training in St. Pete did not get the same attention as Yankee Stadium in New York (the "House that Ruth Built"), St. Petersburg still got its share of baseball theatrics. In the 1930 season, Colonel Jacob Ruppert landed on the practice field at Crescent Lake on the Goodyear blimp *Vigilant* to deliver baseball bats to Babe Ruth and other team members. "Men with ropes dragged [the blimp] until its cabin was near the pitchers' box, where Colonel Ruppert disembarked, closely followed by the bats." (Al Lang Stadium is called the "Other House that Ruth Built.") In 1928, some 270,000 fans saw the Yankees in spring training. It is said that the population of St. Pete tripled when Ruth was playing baseball here.

In addition to playing baseball, Ruth was an inveterate golfer. When asked about all the golf he played, he said that he did it to help keep his weight down. "You see, divot-digging and slicing the white-washed walnuts keeps the avoirdupois down." Local resident Bill Cooper remembered as a boy caddying for Ruth at the Jungle. Ruth did not play very well that day and ended up smashing his club against a pine tree and saying a few "harsh words." Bill remembered Ruth as a "big kidder." Ruth shot close to pro level, and as one would expect, his driving was frequently world class. He

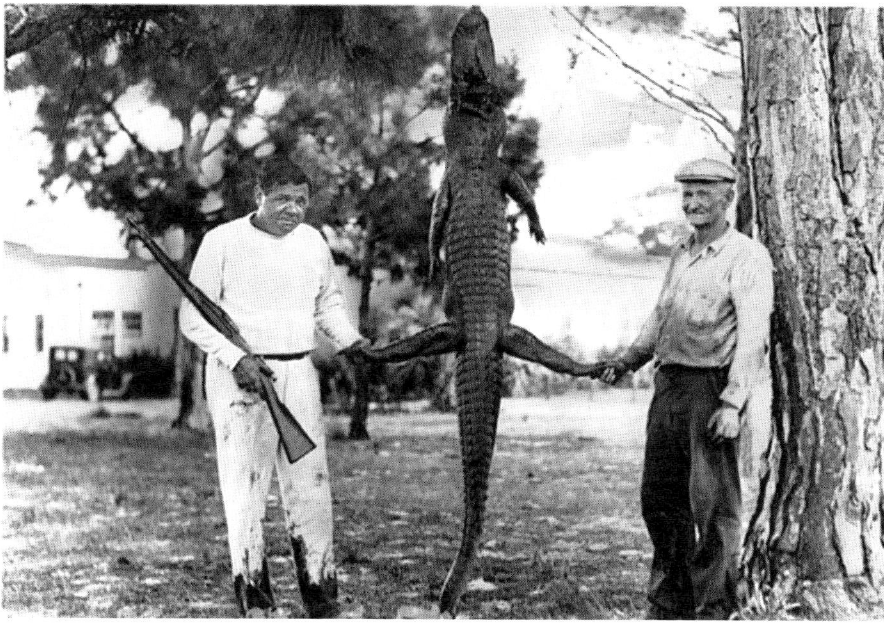

Babe Ruth alligator hunting in the St. Petersburg area. *Courtesy Linda Ruth Tosetti.*

once broke the world distance drive record. One of his close golfing buddies was the cartoonist and St. Pete resident Billy De Beck (*Barney Google*). As *St. Petersburg Times* writer Jeff Klinkenberg once wrote of the Babe, "He loved it here. He loved our weather, especially when it was sunny, when he could sneak out in the morning before practice and play golf. He loved our courses, especially the wide fairways that could contain his mighty drives. He was a lousy putter; the man didn't know his strength and sometimes threw his club in disgust when the ball rolled past the cup. But he laughed afterward."

"I HAD A BETTER YEAR"

During the 1930 season, Ruth and his wife, Claire, arrived in St. Petersburg in January. He played golf with former governor and presidential candidate Al Smith, who was vacationing in Florida. He was judge at a heavyweight fight, giving the decision to Big Jeff Carroll over Bert Finch, a St. Petersburg fireman. He went quail shooting and shot a rattlesnake dead in the head when it poised to strike. That season saw Ruth make $80,000. The deal was made with Yankees owner Colonel Jake Ruppert at the Princess Martha Hotel. $80,000 was $5,000 more than President Hoover made at the time. There is a story (probably untrue) about Ruth being asked if he should really be making more than the president of the United States. He replied, "Well, I had a better year than he did."

In 1932, Ruth took a $5,000 pay cut. Ruth's $80,000 salary was out of place in the depths of the Great Depression. His new reduced salary was also contracted in St. Petersburg, this time at the Rolyat Hotel. He and Ruppert signed the new contract in front of a wishing well. Ruth and Claire then tossed coins in the well for luck. Babe wished for a Yankee pennant. Claire for two more $75,000 contracts. Colonel Ruppert asked for the money in the wishing well. Ruth then tossed in an extra silver half dollar. "There goes some of this year's contract," he said.

Claire did not get her wish. Seventeen days after President Roosevelt closed the nation's banks to stop bank runs, Ruth's salary was drastically reduced. For the 1933 season, he signed a contract for $52,000, and once again the contract signing was in St. Pete.

A SOFT SPOT FOR KIDS

Having been abandoned by his family as a small child, Ruth always had a soft spot for kids. From the day Ruth set foot in St. Pete, he was exceptionally generous to local kids. In March 1925, right near the time of his initial arrival in town, a mom and dad were killed in an accident on the new Gandy Bridge. Babe led a campaign to financially help their orphaned children through appearances at theaters and other locations.

St. Petersburg native Ardith Rutland remembered as a little girl selling orange juice and peanut butter sandwiches on a fairway at the Belleview Biltmore's golf course. Up comes the Babe. "What's your name, Mister?" "I'm Babe Ruth." Ardith considered that for a minute and then said, "If you're Babe Ruth, where's your candy bars?" The next day, the Babe presented her with a Baby Ruth candy bar. Ardith said, "Just one! My uncle brings me two!" Not to be outdone, the following day the Babe brought her a whole box! Ardith remembered him as a Santa Claus–like person dressed in what she called at the time "shorts" (knickers). Ruth himself had

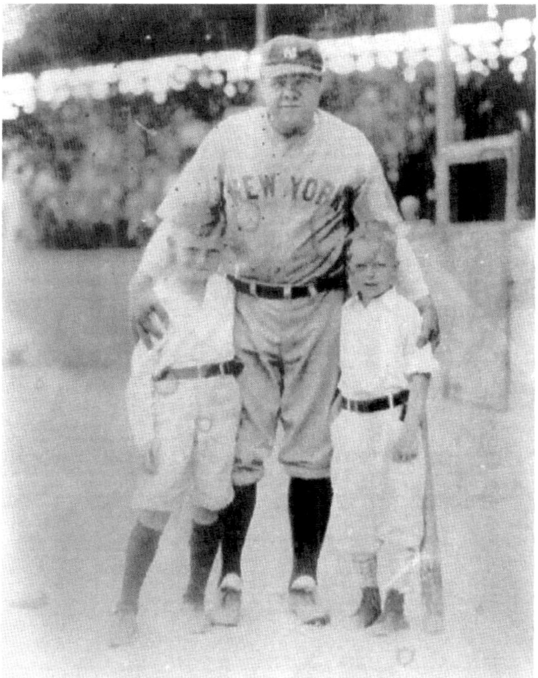

Babe Ruth with batboys Philip Dann and Dan Heistand in St. Petersburg, 1932. *Courtesy St. Petersburg Museum of History.*

nothing to do with Baby Ruth candy bars, other than to unsuccessfully sue the manufacturer for exploiting his name.

In 1934, at the height of the Depression, he organized a project that brought fifty boys as his guests to spring training in St. Pete. The boys traveled first class on the Orange Blossom Special train and stayed at the upscale Huntington Hotel. After the boys left, Ruth shipped each of them a crate of oranges and grapefruit as a remembrance. Ruth enjoyed Florida so much that he returned to St. Petersburg after retirement.

As a kid, Mike Mastry made a business out of Babe Ruth autographed baseballs. Before the games, he would bike over to Kress dime store and buy a dozen baseballs for a quarter each. He would then ride back to Waterfront Park and wait for his chance to approach Ruth for autographs. "He signed my baseballs, and after the game I'd sell them for a dollar each. That was a fortune back then. I thought I was rich." This went on day after day, but Ruth never turned Mike down. "Here, keed" the Babe would say, autographing every ball. "Hey, Babe," some grouch would complain. "The kid is selling those balls and makin' lots of dough off you." "I grew up poor," replied the Babe. "I appreciate a keed that works."

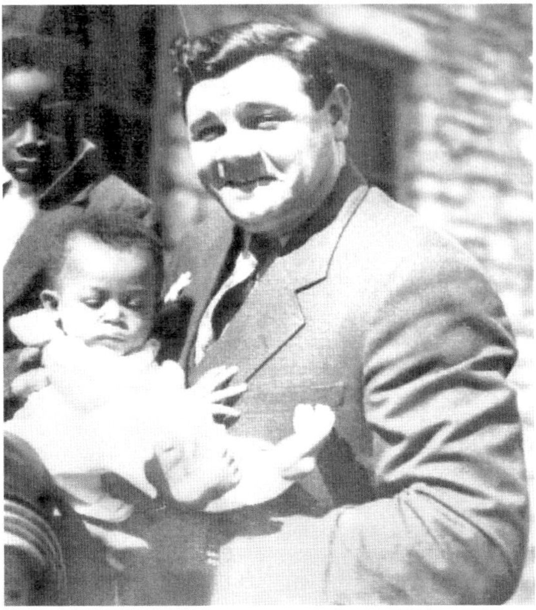

Left: Babe Ruth and one of his youngest fans. *Courtesy Linda Ruth Tosetti.*

Below: Babe Ruth's daughter, Dorothy, accompanied Ruth and her mother, Helen, to spring training in St. Petersburg. Photo taken at Waterfront Park in St. Petersburg, 1925. *Courtesy Linda Ruth Tosetti.*

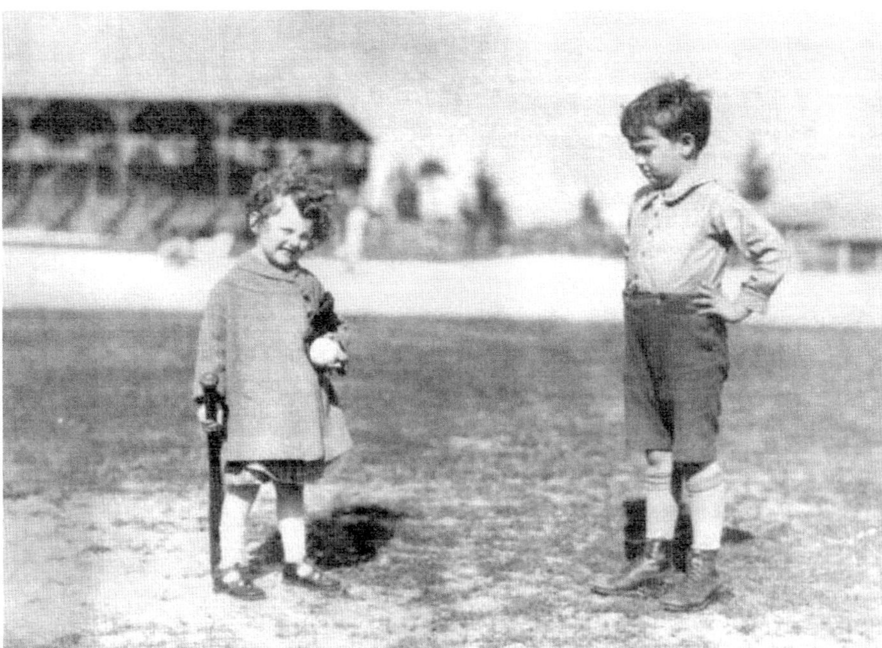

Lois Laughner Sullivan remembered that her first husband, Paul Laughner, had fond memories of the Babe from his youth. As a kid, Paul knew Ruth well. Ruth frequently visited the Vinoy Hotel, built in 1925 by Paul's father, Aymer Vinoy Laughner. Ruth loved to play with Paul and other children, often getting down on his knees to do so. Harry F. Woods remembered a story about having dinner with a friend of the Woods family and Babe Ruth when a group of young boys gathered outside the house on their bicycles. The Babe went outside to talk with the boys and somehow wound up on one of the bikes. Apparently, his bicycle skills were not as good as his baseball skills. He rolled the bike into nearby Crescent Lake. On another occasion, Ruth was driving back from playing golf at Pasadena Golf and Country Club when he spotted a group of kids playing baseball in a sandlot. He couldn't resist giving the kids a thrill and had the driver stop. He pitched to each boy, allowing an easy hit. That way, he said, it would give them something to pass on to their grandchildren—that they each got a hit off the Babe.

Babe's daughter, Dorothy, accompanied Babe and her mother, Helen, to spring training until Helen's separation from Babe in 1926. While visiting St. Pete with Babe and Helen, Dorothy attended the Aiken Open Air School, previously on the site of Presbyterian Towers near the Old Northeast neighborhood. She was the darling of the Yankees and traveled with the team to and from spring training. Many years later, when Ruth was first told about his cancer, Dorothy was there. She recalled, "I just wanted to throw my arms around him and tell him how much he meant to me."

In the late 1920s, the Yankees played the Reds in an exhibition game in nearby Tampa. Right before the game, a car drove up to the right field foul line and parked. In it were a father and his very sick son, there to see the game from a good vantage point. After the game, the players jogged by the car to their bus for the return trip to St. Pete. As Ruth jogged by, he shouted out, "Hi'ya kid" to the boy in the car. The boy struggled to his feet and called out something to the Babe. The boy's father was amazed and kept repeating, "My boy stood up! My boy stood up! This is the first time in two years that my boy has stood up." Such was Ruth's power of inspiration to America's young people.

Ruth worked tirelessly for local charitable causes. He visited hospitals, raised funds for civic projects and made endless appearances at fundraising events for organizations such as the Kids and Kubs and the Woman's Club. He spoke and coached at the new St. Petersburg High School, which opened in 1926. In 1928, he helped lead an American Legion fund drive to establish

Crippled Children's Hospital (now All Children's Hospital). "I really feel it more a privilege than a duty to do what little I can to help keep up the good work that is being done here by the [America] Legion and the citizens of St. Petersburg," he said. In 1930, he helped raise funds to pay the interest on the YMCA. Although no longer used as a YMCA, the building still remains as a designated local landmark. It is noted for its exemplary Mediterranean Revival–style architecture. His support was pivotal for the success of such an ambitious project in the depths of the Depression. After he retired, he championed help for veterans, sold war bonds and was recognized for his efforts by being made an honorary commandant of the Florida Military Academy (formerly the Rolyat Hotel).

Was Ruth's charitable work genuine or just good PR? Ruth himself once said, "Don't misunderstand me. I'm not trying to pretend that we—the players—have any altruistic mission in life. Frankly, as you may have guessed, we play baseball for a living—it's our job. And yet, I do believe that we accomplish more than just our own selfish purpose." Babe's granddaughter, Linda Ruth Tosetti, reflected, "I think what my mom, Dorothy, learned from her dad wherever he went, including the years she shared going to St. Petersburg, was all the giving back to people that Babe did. She was aware of the hospitals, the schools, the orphanages he visited…the people he helped. It was instilled in her very young, and I am sure it happened starting in St. Petersburg. It is an important part of the legacy she passed on to me."

After Ruth left the Yankees to join the Boston Braves, his ability to attract a crowd was in no way diminished. St. Petersburg's Waterfront Park stadium was built to hold 2,500 people. One day, more than 6,000 people turned out to see Ruth play. This was his last spring training season in a twenty-two-year career as an active player. After retiring from major league baseball in 1936, Ruth bought a winter beachfront home on nearby Treasure Island.

NINTH INNING

Ruth, the Yankees and his teammates, including such stars as Lou Gehrig and Tony Lazerri, brought fame to St. Petersburg and served as a major force in attracting tourists. As Mayor Lang reflected, "The Yankees with Babe Ruth and their stars meant millions to this town." City council member

Elon (E.C) Robison said, "The greatest single factor in St. Petersburg's becoming a city of really major proportions has been baseball."

But what of Ruth himself? Baseball writer Red Smith once wrote, "The man was a boy, simple, artless, genuine and unabashed. This explains his rapport with children, whom he met as intellectual equals." Tommy Holmes, a major league player and later baseball writer, stated, "Some 20 years ago, I stopped talking about the Babe for the simple reason that I realized that those who had never seen him didn't believe me." Babe loved St. Petersburg and fully embraced its lifestyle, and he greatly magnified the city's association with sports, outdoor leisure and just plain fun. He significantly contributed to its sense of place.

NOTE ON DOROTHY RUTH

Babe Ruth was married to Helen Woodford in 1914 at the age of nineteen. She was sixteen. She and Ruth separated in 1926, and Helen perished in a fire in 1929. Ruth married Claire Hodgson in 1929 after Helen's death. Claire died in 1976. Claire had a twelve-year-old daughter by her first husband whom Ruth adopted. Claire's daughter's name was Julia. Julia now lives in Arizona.

Ruth's first daughter was named Dorothy. According to Linda Ruth Tosetti, Babe Ruth's granddaughter, Dorothy was born in 1921 to Babe and his girlfriend, Juanita Jennings Ellias of California. Dorothy was raised by Babe and Helen Ruth until Babe separated from Helen. Dorothy lived with Helen after the separation.

After Helen's death, Dorothy was raised by Babe and Claire Hodgson. Dorothy died in 1989. Babe Ruth's granddaughter, Linda Ruth Tosetti, is the youngest of six children born to Babe's daughter, Dorothy Ruth Pirone. Linda lives in Connecticut.

Sources used in this chapter include Marty Apple, *Pinstripe Empire*; Raymond Arsenault, *St. Petersburg and the Florida Dream*; James W. Covington, "Babe Ruth and His Record 'Home Run" at Tampa," *Sunland Tribune*; Walter P. Fuller, *St. Petersburg and Its People*; Karl H. Grismer, *The Story of St. Petersburg*; Jeff Klinkenberg, "Thanks Babe"; Kevin McCarthy, *Babe Ruth in Florida* and *Baseball in Florida*; Will Michaels, "Babe Ruth in St. Pete," *Northeast*

Journal, 2009; Leigh Montville, *The Big Bam*; *St. Petersburg Times*; *New York Times* (especially March 8, 1920, page 10); Tampa Bay Rays, "Rays History," tampabay.rays.mlb.com/tb_history_tampabay.jsp; Tim Reid and the Committee to Commemorate Babe Ruth; Dorothy Ruth, *My Dad, the Babe*; and interviews with Bill Cooper, Ardith Rultand, Lois Laughner Sullivan, Harry F. Woods and Linda Ruth Tosetti.

St. Pete's First Entertainment Centers

Hard Acts to Follow

In the 1920s, St. Petersburg had less than 27,000 people, but it boasted unbelievable performing arts venues for such a small city. Among these were La Plaza Theatre, the Coliseum and the Manhattan Casino. While George S. Gandy is best known for building the Gandy Bridge in 1924, the first bridge linking Tampa Bay between Tampa and St. Petersburg, this was not his first remarkable St. Petersburg enterprise. Eleven years before this, "Dad" Gandy, as he was affectionately called, built another imposing structure called La Plaza Theatre. The La Plaza was opened on March 8, 1913. It cost $150,000. The theater seated an astounding 1,800 people—a figure that represented 25 percent of the city's 7,000 permanent population at the time. Small wonder that many people thought the theater was way beyond what a small city like St. Petersburg could support. It was referred to as "Gandy's White Elephant." However, the white elephant soon became the golden goose. After a few lean startup years, it became profitable.

The first performance was Cammaranos's *Il Trovatore*, performed by the Royal Italian Company. During the winter months, La Plaza offered stage shows featuring major performers such as the Russian ballerina Anna Pavlova, the cowboy Tom Mix and singer Sophie Tucker. Even John Philip Sousa's band played there. St. Petersburg High School graduations were also held there. In 1920, La Plaza became largely a film theater.

George Gandy was a self-made man who grew up in Philadelphia. He began work as an office boy working for Henry Disston & Sons, the famous saw manufacturing company. This is the same Disston family who purchased millions of acres of Florida real estate and founded Disston City, now known as Gulfport. From there, Gandy became involved in railroads, trolleys and theaters. His granddaughter, Helen Gandy O'Brien, recalled that he built three theaters in the Philadelphia area before coming to St. Petersburg to live in 1908. Helen stated that at the time La Plaza was built, it was the biggest theater south of Atlanta. When asked why Gandy built the La Plaza, Helen stated that her grandfather thought that "St. Pete needed a little dash of culture."

The Plaza Theatre complex, located at the southwest corner of Fifth Street and Central Avenue, was built in phases that finally took on the shape of a "U." The theater was the largest of the three units making up the complex. Two wings faced Central Avenue. For a short time, the Gandy family lived on the second floor of one of these wings. Offices and stores occupied the remainder of the wings. Helen's parents were George S. Gandy Jr., known as "Gidge," and Edith Brooks Gandy. As with the later Gandy Bridge project, Gandy heavily relied on his sons Gidge and Al to manage the La Plaza enterprise. This included traveling to New York City to book the best vaudeville acts and plays. But Gidge would also run the light board and take on small parts in the play. Gidge also later founded the historic St. Petersburg–Havana Sailboat Races, now known as the Southern Ocean Racing Conference.

Despite the fact that Helen's dad managed the theater, he and Helen's mother were very protective of her and careful only to allow her to see the "right kind" of shows and films at the La Plaza. On one occasion, she remembered that she was allowed to see *Little Orphan Annie*. However, the performance turned out to be a double header, and the second feature was not something that her parents would have let her see had they known. Helen remembered it as one of the most "terrifying" movies she ever saw. She also recalled watching the Festival of the States Parade from her father's office at La Plaza.

In 1935, a petition was submitted to the city council signed by a few African American residents questioning La Plaza's policy of allowing African Americans into a downtown theater. The petition noted that "the existence of the Harlem Theatre, which caters to the colored race was being threatened due to the fact that colored people are allowed to attend [La] Plaza Theatre, and requested that an ordinance be passed restricting theaters catering to colored people, to the Negro District." La Plaza was the only downtown theater that allowed African Americans to view movies at that time. However, they were restricted to the balcony. The balcony was high in the rear of the theater and was reached by a steep stairway from Fifth Street and a separate box office. White patrons entered from Central Avenue. In 1948, La Plaza was acquired by the Florida State Theaters. It was demolished in 1957. In its heyday, it served as a city cultural center and predated the Coliseum by eleven years.

THE COLISEUM

While La Plaza gave the city a major theater, it still lacked a major dance hall. The Coliseum opened on November 20, 1924, the same day as the opening of the Gandy Bridge. It was one of the nation's busiest dance halls and was described as "St. Petersburg's Palace of Pleasure." One local woman armed with religious pamphlets routinely stood outside the entrance to warn patrons that they were about to enter a den of sin.

The Coliseum was built by a group of Detroit businessmen led by C.F. Cullen. The architect was T.H. Eslick. The exterior was Mediterranean Revival/Moorish in style, but the interior looked like a giant Quonset hut. It had 1,800 square feet of maple floor, balcony seating for 450 people, a large L-shaped soda fountain, eight loges for private seating and a "Rotary Jewel" covered with mirrors that rotated from the ceiling while eight spotlights shined on it. The Coliseum was patterned after a famous amusement center near Los Angeles known as "Somewhere in France." Its cost was $250,000. The local *Tourist News* called the Coliseum "the largest and finest" dance hall south of Washington, D.C.

On opening night, Mayor R.S. Pearce and three thousand guests danced to the music of the Florida Four, a Jacksonville quartet. The *Times* reported, "Women in furs and men in tuxedos glided under the tinseled chandeliers and the high vaulted ceiling as jazz musicians played 'Tuxedo Junction,' 'Night Train,' and 'As Time Goes By' on a stage built to look like a medieval castle." Those attending paid two dollars for a table, ten cents for sodas and fifteen cents for pie—à la mode cost ten cents more. In 1926, a local twenty-one-year-old banjo player, Rex MacDonald, formed the Silver Kings band. The group became regulars throughout the 1920s.

All winter long, fans of the foxtrot and Charleston danced to the music of local bands such as the Tom Danks Orchestra or Rex MacDonald's Silver Kings. Celebrated big-band leaders such as Paul Whiteman, Harry James,

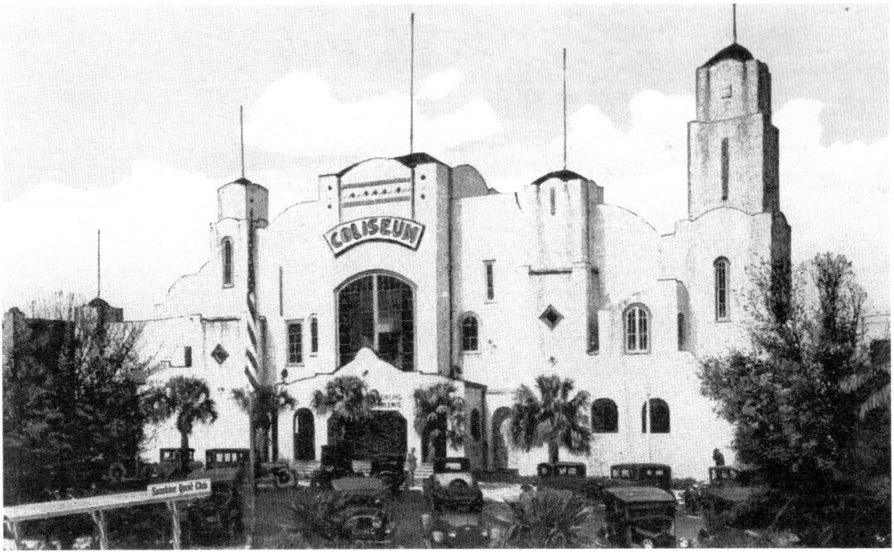

The Coliseum opened in 1924 and was billed as "St. Petersburg's Palace of Pleasure." Entertainers ranged from Duke Ellington to Will Rogers. The Coliseum continues to thrive today and is a city historic landmark. *Courtesy City of St. Petersburg.*

Benny Goodman, Guy Lombardo and Count Basie also performed, as did humorist Will Rogers and evangelist Aimee Semple McPherson. In 1945, Sammy Kaye set an attendance record by drawing 3,300 fans. Even radio shows were broadcast from the dance floor, including *Ted Mack's Original Amateur Hour* and *Don McNeils's Breakfast Club*. The Boston Celtics played an exhibition game in the 1930s. But this was not just a venue for big name performers. On one occasion, the local Lion's Club sponsored a horned toad race. In the 1960s, several tennis exhibitions were scheduled, including stars such as Poncho Segura, Jack Kramer and Bobby Riggs. In 1985, the film *Cocoon* shot dance scenes in the Casino. The early artists performed without the benefit of a microphone. Amplification was not installed until 1932.

While "Duke" Ellington and other African Americans performed at the Coliseum, African Americans were barred from attending until desegregation began in the 1960s. In 1956, Louis Armstrong backed out of a gig at the Coliseum "because it was all for the whites." Cab Calloway required stitches when he was struck with a bottle by a white patron because he was hugged by a white female fan.

The Coliseum never closed, even during the Depression of the 1930s. In 1945, Rex MacDonald, his wife and an associate purchased the Coliseum for a reported $75,000. MacDonald was elected to the city council in the mid-1950s. From 1945 until his death in 1984, the banjo player turned owner and promoter, with his wife, Boo MacDonald, scheduled decades of St. Petersburg's finest entertainment and expositions. In 1989, Boo MacDonald sold the Coliseum to the city for $824,500. Among the improvements made by the city was a 15,525-square-foot red oak floor placed over the original white maple flooring. The Coliseum continued to be an important city-designated historic landmark, as well as an active entertainment and culture center. This is historic preservation at its best. Recent events included a rally held for Democratic presidential candidate John Kerry and Mayor Rick Baker's mayoral inaugural ball, the first inaugural ball ever to be held for a mayor in St. Pete.

Manhattan Casino

In 1925, a year after the Coliseum opened, Elder Jordan built the Jordan Dance Hall, later known as the Manhattan Casino, on Twenty-second Avenue South. ("Elder" was his first name, not a title.) Jordon came to the city in 1904. Along with his five sons, he became a prominent African American builder, developer and entrepreneur. He also established a successful bus line. He donated the land for Jordan Elementary School, named in his honor.

African Americans were denied use of the Coliseum and most other entertainment centers, with the exception of the La Plaza, which allowed them use of the balcony popularly known as the "crow's nest." Referred to as the "Gem of 22nd Street" and the "Home of the Happy Feet," the Manhattan Casino became the cultural and social center for the city's African Americans. It was located on the main thoroughfare of the African American community, Twenty-second Street South, popularly called "the Deuces." "One of the beauties of 22nd Street," said Rosalie Peck who grew up in what is now called Midtown, was that "it was the one place in town where you didn't feel the pressure of being a black person, being segregated, treated differently or looked at differently." Most African Americans idealized New York City as a national African American cultural center free of legal segregation. The Manhattan Casino is believed to have been named after this ideal place—the closest thing St. Petersburg had to the Big Apple. Despite its name, there was no gambling.

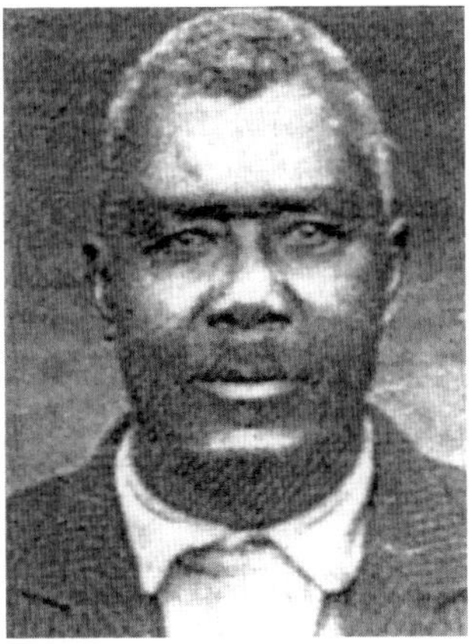

Elder Jordan Sr. built the Manhattan Casino on "the Deuces" and was a leading entrepreneur in the development of the Twenty-Second Street South business center and neighborhood. *Courtesy St. Petersburg Museum of History.*

While Elder Jordan built the Casino, George Grogan promoted it. Grogan was a booking agent covering all of Florida for Universal Attractions in New York. In addition to his booking job, Grogan was simultaneously a chemistry teacher at Gibbs High School. Entertainers who performed there were icons in American performing arts, the caliber of entertainers one would expect to find in New York, Chicago or St. Louis, not a small town like St. Petersburg. They included such celebrities as B.B. King, Cab Calloway, Louis Armstrong, Ray Charles, Nat King Cole, Count Basie, Fats Domino, the Ink Spots, Duke Ellington, Little Richard, Otis Redding, Big Ma Maybelle, Dizzy Gillespie and Della Reese. In addition to Grogan, another booking agent was Reverend Goldie Thompson, a local minister and radio personality. He brought gospel acts such as Shirley Caesar and the Mighty Clouds of Joy to the Casino. Virtually every big African American entertainer performed there. It was considered a select spot on the southern "Chitlin Circuit."

But the Manhattan was not just played by national and international celebrities; it was also a venue for St. Petersburg's own talented musicians, such as Al Downing, Al Williams and George Cooper, who organized the first big African American band in the city. Others included Jerome, Jimmy and Carl Brown; Joe Clark; Horace Cooper; Clayton Fillyau; Robert Harris; William Dandy; Louise Lavine; Elsie Dorn McGarrah; and Willis Wilson. These St. Pete musicians and others kept the music going when the big names were not there.

One local musician who remembered the Manhattan fondly is LeRoy Flemmings Jr.:

> *It had a wooden floor. The building vibrated. Every artist that you could imagine came there. People were crushing against you. We were under age, 14 or 15. To see those guys playing in their favorite clothes, just looking crazy…We would talk about how we were gonna do that. Every now and then the guys would come in the dressing room and they would talk to us*

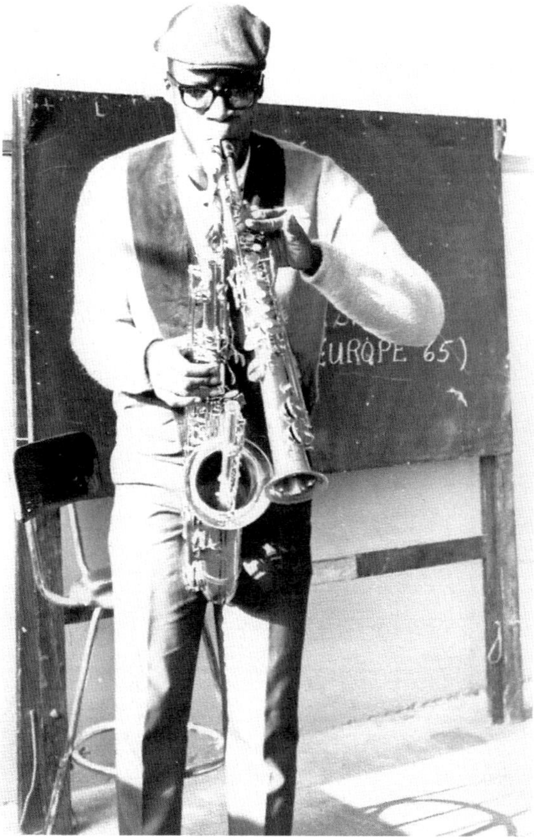

LeRoy Flemmings Jr. played tenor saxophone for James Brown, Otis Redding and Joe Tex. He was discovered by James Brown while Brown was playing at the Manhattan Casino. *Courtesy LeRoy Flemmings Jr.*

> *about your skills and tell about all the great places they went and how many beautiful women there were, and all this madness you know. And I wanted to do this so badly.*

LeRoy was to get his wish. At the age of nineteen, he got a tip that James Brown was in town and needed a sax player. That same day, he auditioned for the gig and, two hours later, was on a bus leaving with Brown's band. Flemmings later performed with Otis Redding and Joe Tex. Flemmings was one of many local black musicians who went on to play and perform with nationally recognized musicians.

But the Manhattan was more than an entertainment center; it was also a meeting place for the African American community—a cultural and social center. The Casino was on the second floor. Shops and a branch post office were on the first floor. There were windows all the way around the building so you could see what was going on in the street below. There were no chairs; however, there were benches lining the walls. The Manhattan was not air conditioned, but there was a porch on the rear of the Casino where patrons could get some air. Admission for dances was twenty-five cents per person. Members of unions were admitted free for local performances, but for out-of-town shows, they had to pay like anyone else. According to Elsie McGarrah, a frequent patron at the Manhattan, the dance floor was so crowded "you couldn't get a match box in there." A bouncer was employed to keep freeloaders from sneaking in. Those who could not afford to pay the twenty-five-cent entrance fee listened outside the windows. The building shook like an earthquake from all the fancy stepping. The stage was so close to the dance floor that you could reach out and touch the performers. And when the "greats" came to town, they invited local amateurs to perform with them.

When Duke Ellington played at the Coliseum, and immediately afterward at the Manhattan, it was for the last time. Since all the hotels in St. Petersburg were segregated, there was no place for him to stay, other than the homes and shops of local African Americans. In frustration, he declared that he would never come to St. Petersburg again. Many other African American performers, including B.B. King, had the same complaint. The Manhattan Casino closed in 1968, an unanticipated consequence of desegregation. The Bayfront Center opened in 1965 drawing away much of the talent that had once performed at the Manhattan. And big name entertainers no longer had to rely on the Chitlin Circuit stops for an income. The Manhattan Casino building was later acquired by the city, preserved and designated an historic landmark. It has been refurbished and is now awaiting willing entrepreneurs to lease it. Perhaps once again its second floor will reverberate with the sounds of jazz, dance and gospel.

The La Plaza, the Coliseum and the Manhattan Casino were followed years later by such venues as the Bayfront Center, the Mahaffey Theater, the Palladium and Studio 620. They set high standards for excellence in entertainment that today's performing arts venues are challenged to meet. They are hard acts to follow.

Sources used in this chapter included Raymond Arsenault, *St. Petersburg and the Florida Dream, 1888–1950*; Walter P. Fuller, *St. Petersburg and Its People*; Karl H. Grismer, *The Story of St. Petersburg*; Scott Hartzell, *Voices of America: St. Petersburg*; Will Michaels, "St. Pete's First Entertainment Centers: Hard Acts to Follow!" *Northeast Journal*, 2006; Rosalie Peck and Jon Wilson, *St. Petersburg's Historic 22nd Street South*; Sandra W. Rooks, *Black America Series: St. Petersburg,*

Florida; Jon Wilson, "The Dueces," *St. Petersburg Times*, July 28, 2002; WSPF TV, "Remembering the Manhattan Casino"; interview with Helen Gandy O'Brien, granddaughter of George S. Gandy Sr.; St. Petersburg Museum of History; and Carter G. Woodson Museum of African American History.

The Grand Hotels of St. Petersburg

Mainstays of the 1920s Boom

Hotels and St. Petersburg's growth have gone hand in hand since the very beginning. Without the hotels, St. Petersburg's tourist and development economy would not have happened. While the hotels themselves provided employment to thousands of local residents, more importantly they provided employment for a great many others working in a wide range of other local business enterprises also patronized by tourists. St. Petersburg's first hotel was the Detroit. Built by Peter Demens, this forty-room hotel was intended to help jump-start development of the city and the use of his Orange Belt Railway. Starting in July 1889, the Orange Belt Railway sponsored seaside tours to exotic and healthful St. Petersburg. Advertisements in northern newspapers featured the Detroit Hotel along with Dr. W.C. Van Bibber's famous 1885 report declaring St. Petersburg's climate as the healthiest in the world.

As the popularity of St. Petersburg as a tourist destination began to build, soon the Detroit, along with a number of lesser hotels, was no longer able to accommodate the inflow of visitors. By 1920, matters had come to a head when several visiting families pitched tents at the corner of Eighteenth Street and Second Avenue South. St. Petersburg's mayor, Noel Mitchell, decided to turn the city's acute hotel shortage into a publicity stunt by not only affirming the decision of these families to pitch their tents but also offering a free campsite to any other tourist who wished to join them. No less than 120 additional families took the offer. These families and others like them came to be known as the "tin can tourists," a sobriquet derived from the canned food they ate over open fires.

While Mitchell was enthusiastic about Tent City, other city leaders were not. They were concerned about St. Pete acquiring a low-end reputation. A common joke of the times was that "the St. Petersburg tourist arrived with one shirt and a $20 bill and never changed either all winter." Tin can tourists were not the kind of tourists they wanted, so Tent City was closed as a public campsite. However, local private entrepreneurs stepped in to offer alternative camps, and these became the forerunners of Florida's mobile home parks.

Aside from the Detroit, other early hotels of note included the Poinsettia, frequented by salesmen; the Floronton; the West Coast Inn, considered a "health spa" because the guests drank from the nearby "Fountain of Youth" still located at First Street and Fourth Avenue South; and the Huntington, which marketed to the well-to-do. The St. Petersburg Museum of History houses a large mural from the Huntington painted by renowned local artist Mark Dixon Dodd.

During the 1920s, though, hotel construction truly began with a vengeance. During this period, no less than eleven new major hotels were constructed in St. Pete and nearby areas. These included the Ponce de Leon (1922), the Soreno (1924), the Suwanee (1924), the Pheil (later named the Madison, started in 1916 and completed in 1924), the Mason (later named the Princess Martha, 1924), the Pennsylvania, the Dennis, the Vinoy Park (1925), the Jungle Country Club Hotel (1925), the Rolyat (1926) and the Don Ce-Sar (1928).

The Soreno was built by Mr. and Mrs. Soren Lund, natives of Denmark, and designed by Atlanta architect G.L. Preacher in the Mediterranean Revival style. Advertised as the city's first million-dollar hotel, it remained one of the fine downtown waterfront hotels for many years until it was imploded in 1992 for the movie *Lethal Weapon 3* starring Mel Gibson. The Pheil was built by former Mayor Abe Pheil (the same Pheil who was first passenger on the world's first airline). A man who loathed debt, Pheil refused to borrow, and that is why a building begun in 1916 was not completed until 1924. He operated a theater on the first floor. Because of his fear of fire, he placed the screen in the area of the front entrance. Moviegoers had to walk under the screen in order to enter and exit. The projection room, with its highly flammable film, was located in a special room built behind the rear main fire wall of the hotel. The Mason was the only hotel that started with public ownership through sale of stock. The hotel was first named the Mason after Franklin J. Mason, the contractor and a principal owner. It was designed by F. Jonsberg of Boston and is in the Neoclassical style. Later, it was acquired by William Muir, who renamed the hotel after his wife, Martha.

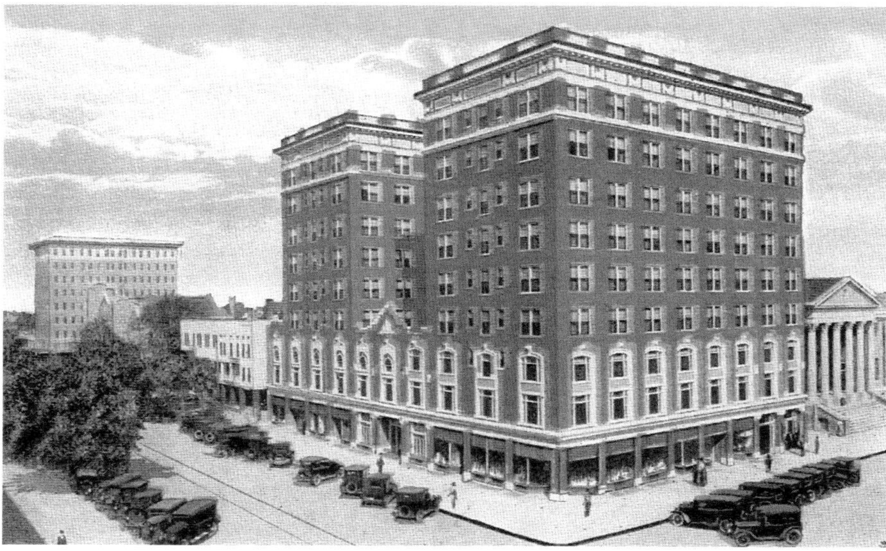

The Mason Hotel, later named the Princess Martha, was constructed in 1924. The hotel was designed by F. Jonsberg of Boston in the Neoclassical style. The Suwanee Hotel is seen to the left and the First Baptist Church to the right. E.C. Kropp Company, Milwaukee. *Courtesy Michaels Family Collection.*

The Vinoy was built by Aymer Vinoy Laughner. It was said to be launched in connection with a wager made between Laughner and early golf champion Walter Hagen. At a party at Laughner's house on Beach Drive near the present site of the Vinoy, Laughner had bet Hagen that he could not hit golf balls off the top of Laughner's watch without breaking the crystal. Hagen won the wager. When Laughner and another guest went to retrieve the golf balls from the neighbor's lawn, the guest commented on what a nice site the waterfront home would be for a hotel. The rest is hotel history. The hotel, with its Mediterranean Revival architecture, was designed by Henry L. Taylor. It was the largest and most luxurious of St. Petersburg's boom-era hotels. The Vinoy came to be famous for its gourmet cuisine and famous guests. Sometimes these did not always go together. An early visitor was former president Calvin Coolidge, known for his simple tastes. According to hotel lore, he preferred to eat in the employees' cafeteria rather than in the hotel's fine restaurants. The film *The Break* with Vince Van Patten was filmed at the Vinoy in 1995.

The Rolyat was built by "Handsome Jack" Taylor, a northeastern investment banker and husband of the Delaware heiress Evelyn DuPont. These two high rollers developed the area of Pasadena and topped it off

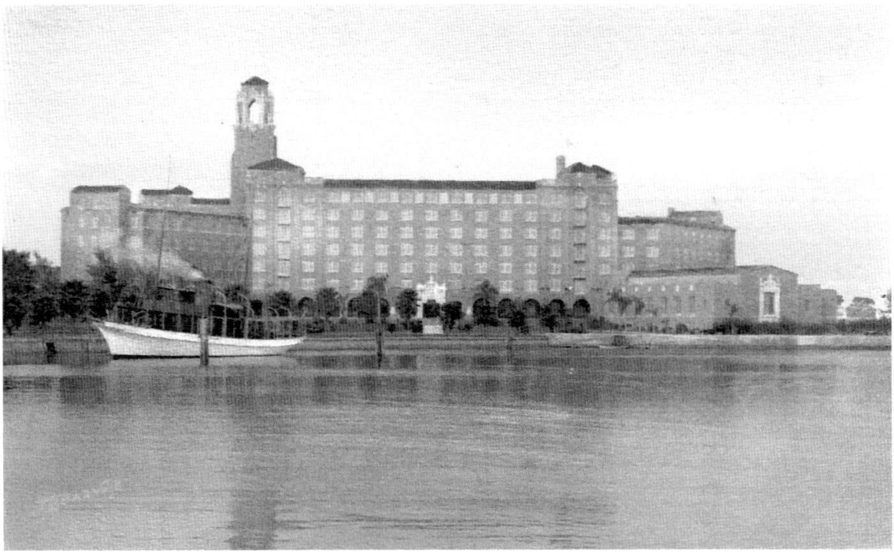

The Vinoy Park Hotel was built in 1925 and designed by Henry L. Taylor in the Mediterranean Revival style. Barnhill photographed St. Petersburg between 1914 and 1930. Before coming to St. Petersburg, he worked with renowned western photographer Edward Curtis. Curtis trained Barnhill in use of his famous gold toning process, giving his photos a golden glow. Barnhill's postcards are highly collectable. E.G. Barnhill, St. Petersburg, hand-colored. *Courtesy Michaels Family Collection.*

with the Spanish Revival–style Rolyat Hotel designed by Richard Kiehnel of Miami. Opening night saw a lavish party attended by Babe Ruth, Walter Hagen (who was also president of Taylor's Pasadena Golf and Country Club), August Heckscher and many other celebrities. On one occasion, Evelyn DuPont sealed a local real estate deal by rolling down her stockings to reveal one of several hidden $10,000 bills. Since 1954, the Rolyat Hotel has been the site of Stetson Law School. In 1957, the film *The Strange One*, starring Ben Gazzara and George Peppard, was filmed at this location.

The Don Ce-Sar, at Pass-a-Grille, was built by Thomas J. Rowe. Rowe was originally from Ireland and had lived in Norfolk, Virginia, before arriving in Pinellas. He named the hotel for his favorite grand opera character, Don Caesar DeBazan from Vincent Wallace's *Maritana*. The hotel is designed with a blend of Mediterranean and Moorish themes. Guests included F. Scott and Zelda Fitzgerald (F. Scott wrote about the hotel in his novel *Crack-Up*), Clarence Darrow, the Bloomingdales, the Gimbels and the New York Yankees, who used the hotel as their training headquarters in the 1930s. The Don has been the location for such films as *Once Upon a Time in America* with

Robert De Niro, *Forever Mine* with Ray Liotta, *Thunder in Paradise* with Hulk Hogan and *Health* with Lauren Bacall. (The hyphen in the Don's name was later dropped by Bill Bowman, who purchased the Don in 1972). The Jungle Country Club Hotel was built by Walter P. Fuller and designed by Henry L. Taylor in the Mediterranean Revival style in the Jungle area. It is now the site of the Admiral Farragut Naval Academy.

As historian Raymond Arsenault noted, "[T]he Mediterranean Revival landmarks created during the 1920s added a touch of romantic frivolity that solidified the city's identification with leisure." The hotels of the 1920s added about 2,000 rooms to the accommodations of the community, for a total of about 4,500. They were necessary to sustain the tourist economy. In large measure, it was also the tourist who fed the sale of land. In 1926, the land speculation bubble burst, but the tourists continued to come to St. Petersburg and its hotels, helping to sustain the local economy until the dark days following the 1929 stock market crash.

Tourism began to revive in the mid- and late 1930s, but just as it began to get its legs, World War II came along. Showing their ingenuity, the idea occurred to city leaders to pitch St. Petersburg's extensive network of hotels as housing accommodations to the military. Subsequently, the Army Air Force Technical Training Command housed thousands of soldiers in St. Petersburg's hotels. All were leased with the exception of the Don and the Suwanee. The Suwanee was the sole major hotel set aside for civilian use. The government had to condemn the Don in order to acquire it. It first became a medical facility and later a Veterans Administration office center. The hotels again rescued our local economy. What is more, many military personnel who trained in St. Petersburg returned to live here after the war, or later upon their retirement.

A number of hotels—such as the Alexander, Cordova, Dennis (Williams Park), Detroit, Harlan, Princess Martha, Vinoy, Jungle Country Club, Mari-Jean, Pennsylvania, Ponce de Leon, Rolyat and Sunset—have been designated local historic landmarks. They do not serve as museums but rather continue to operate as hotels or in some cases as schools, condos and retirement facilities. The restoration of the Vinoy in 1992, now the Renaissance Vinoy Resort & Golf Club, is widely credited with sparking the revival of St. Petersburg's downtown. This is historic preservation at its best. These grand and not so grand hotels remain to remind us of an earlier era, as well as the people who visited and came to appreciate our city. These visitors also helped to validate our choice of St. Petersburg as a place to live and raise our families.

Sources used for this article include Raymond Arsenault, *St. Petersburg and the Florida Dream, 1888–1950*; Walter P. Fuller, *St. Petersburg and Its People*; Prudy Taylor Board, *The Renaissance Vinoy: St. Petersburg's Crown Jewel*; Walter Hagen, with Margaret Seaton Heck, *The Walter Hagen Story*; June Hurley, *The Don Ce-Sar Story*; June Hurley Young, *The Vinoy: Faded Glory Renewed*; and Will Michaels, "St. Petersburg's Grand Hotels: Mainstay of the 1920s Boom," *Northeast Journal*, 2004.

Civil Rights

Before the 1950s and 1960s, St. Petersburg's African American community had experienced instances of white mob brutality, a lynching, whites-only primaries designed to minimize the black vote, legally sanctioned segregation and Ku Klux Klan intimidation. At the dawn of the civil rights era, St. Petersburg remained one of the most residentially segregated cities in the nation. Legally sanctioned segregation in neighborhoods did not end until 1968. Hospitals were segregated—whites used Mound Park (now Bayfront), and blacks used Mercy Hospital. Schools were segregated. As discussed in an earlier chapter, baseball was segregated. St. Petersburg's famous green benches offered a place of rest, friendliness and socialization for whites, but blacks were not allowed to sit on them.

In 1953, Dr. Ralph M. Wimbish founded the Ambassadors Club for the purpose of improving living conditions, "working within the system," primarily within the African American community. Other charter members of the club were Dr. Orion Ayer

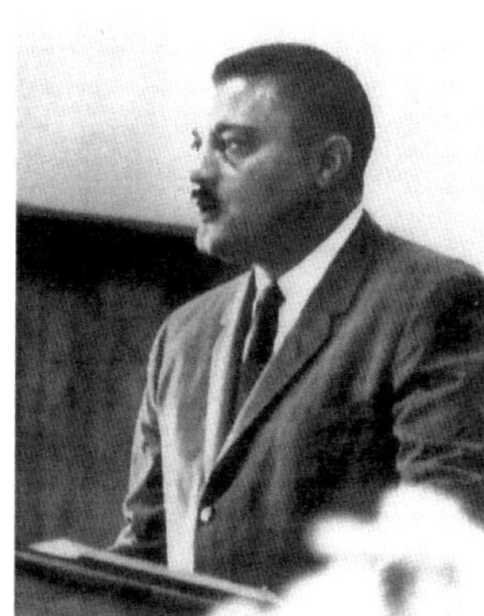

Dr. Ralph Wimbish was a leader in efforts to desegregate Spa Beach and lunch counters, obtain open accommodations for African American baseball players and integrate schools and public golf courses. *Courtesy St. Petersburg Museum of History.*

Sr., Dr. Robert J. Swain, Dr. Fred Alsup, Samuel Blossom, Sidney Campbell, George Grogan, John Hopkins, Ernest Ponder and Emanuel Stewart. Many others would become members of the club over the years. The club's first project was to successfully integrate the Festival of the States Parade. After that, the club's members were involved at some level in nearly all of the various efforts to eliminate segregation and discrimination within the city.

SPA POOL AND BEACH

Integration and extension of civil rights were slow to come in St. Petersburg and Florida. While city libraries were desegregated as early as 1952, desegregation of other facilities took much longer. The first major effort to crack segregation in our city was integration of the beaches and public pools. In St. Petersburg itself, the beaches were small areas on the bay. The major downtown beach was Spa Beach, adjacent to the Spa indoor swimming facility on the north side of the approach to the pier. Historically, this was much larger than it is today and was restricted to whites, as was the pool. In 1916, Mayor Al Lang granted blacks a small piece of beach on Tampa Bay at the South Mole, also known as Demens Landing (foot of First Avenue Southeast).

The beach area was cluttered with rubble, and bathhouse facilities were small. The site was also used for storage by the city. Even there, blacks were cautioned not to swim "in large numbers." Blacks could not legally swim anywhere else along St. Petersburg's forty-five miles of coastline at that time. In the 1930s, whites protested even the use of South Mole by blacks for swimming because blacks had to travel through the segregated white parts of the city to get there. Also, there were no public pools open to blacks. In 1954, Jennie Hall, a retired white schoolteacher, donated money to the city to build the first public pool for blacks. The pool was named after her and is still operating. It was recently designated a city landmark. Jennie Hall was publicly honored by the Ambassadors Club.

In 1954, the U.S. Supreme Court outlawed public school segregation in the *Brown v. Board of Education* decision. This was an impetus to desegregate not only schools but also all public facilities. In St. Petersburg, local direct efforts to desegregate public facilities began with segregated beaches and swimming pools, not schools. In 1955, a local civil rights organization

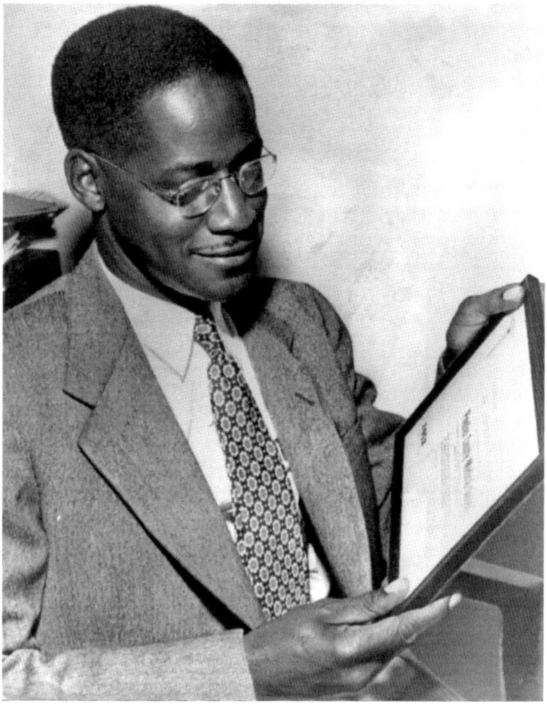

Dr. Fred Alsup, a member of the Ambassadors Club, successfully sued the city to desegregate Spa Beach and Pool. Dr. Alsup was the first African American to be admitted to the Pinellas County Medical Association. He is shown here with his medical society certificate, 1952. *Courtesy St. Petersburg Museum of History.*

called the Civic Coordinating Committee (CCC), led by J.P. Moses, tested segregation at Spa Beach. When CCC members were denied use of the beach, Ambassadors Club member Dr. Fred Alsup filed suit against the city citing violation of their constitutional rights. The courts ruled that the segregation of the beach was unconstitutional. The city tried to undermine the court's ruling by closing the beach anytime persons of color tried to use it and by proposing to build a cultural center or auditorium there. After a long struggle, the beach was finally opened to blacks in 1959. While some black leaders such as Reverend John Wesley Carter of Bethel Metropolitan Baptist Church led bold efforts for better treatment of blacks as early as the 1930s, it was the Civic Coordinating Committee's efforts starting in 1955 that was the beginning of the movement to directly challenge segregation throughout the city.

Buses

Integration of the city's buses occurred in 1959, but black drivers were not hired until 1962. While the heroic Freedom Riders were treated with abuse and brutality in many areas of the South, this was not the case in St. Petersburg. On June 15, 1961, the Freedom Riders made a stop in St. Petersburg and ate at the Greyhound restaurant without incident. One white man did harass Reverend Macdonald Nelson, who was part of a welcoming committee headed by Reverend Enoch Douglas Davis of Bethel Community Baptist Church. The white harasser was arrested. At a workshop later in the day, Freedom Rider Ralph Diamond stated, "We will lose what we've gained if this is not followed up locally. It must get to the point where it will become a natural thing for the two races to sit together at counters."

Lunch Counters

Actually, efforts in St. Petersburg to integrate lunch counters had begun the previous year. Local civil rights leaders including C. Bette Wimbish, Theodore Floyd, J.P. Moses, Reverend Dr. H. McDonald and others conducted sit-ins at various St. Petersburg lunch counters, including Webb's City. In late 1960, the local National Association for the Advancement of Colored People (NAACP), led by Dr. Ralph M. Wimbish, the CCC and the local chapter of the Congress of Racial Equality (CORE), led by attorney Ike Williams and including Ambassadors Club member Emanuel Stewart and David Isom, began a boycott of department stores operating segregated lunch counters. This was done in coordination with a national NAACP effort. Also prominent in these efforts were Reverend Enoch Douglas Davis and the Council of Churches. (Davis was later honored for his leadership in the local civil rights movement when a community center was named for him on Eighteenth Avenue South.)

When an out-of-town Ku Klux Klan wizard tried to make trouble, he was turned away by local Police Chief E. Wilson Purdy. Chief Purdy has been credited for his professionalism in handling the boycott and related picketing. Webb's City obtained a court injunction to stop the boycott. The injunction was quickly appealed by local NAACP lawyers Fred Minnis and Ike Williams.

At the urging of Florida governor LeRoy Collins, the city established the Bi-Racial Committee to try to mediate the situation. On January 3, 1961, fifteen stores in Greater St. Petersburg, including Kress, Maas Bros., Woolworth's and Webb's City, dropped their segregation policies.

Hospitals

Historically, St. Pete had two hospitals—Mound Park, later to become Bayfront, which served whites, and Mercy Hospital built in 1923 for blacks at 1344 Twenty-Second Street South. In 1960, a city task force recommended that a new hospital for blacks be built next to Mound Park, and the city council voted to spend $1.7 million for construction. The all-white Mound Park Hospital Advisory Board opposed the construction. In response, the city council voted to build a new integrated wing at Mound Park and also renovate Mercy Hospital. Mound Park Hospital became integrated in 1961. Mercy Hospital now operates as the Johnnie Ruth Clarke Health Center and is a local landmark. Dr. Fred Alsup, a leader in the efforts to integrate Spa Beach, became the first physician to be accepted as a member of the Pinellas County Medical Society in 1962.

Theaters

As of 1960, five of St. Petersburg's eight movie theaters accepted black patrons on an integrated basis. The three that did not included the Center, State and Florida. On January 11, 1962, members of the NAACP Youth Council, under the leadership of Arnette Doctor, tried to buy tickets to the theaters but were denied. A few white patrons bought tickets for them, but these were not honored. A few days later, ten black young adults were arrested at the Center Theater while attempting to see the movie *King of Kings*, the story of Jesus. Also, NAACP president Leon Cox was fired from his job as a local college teacher, and college student Arnette Doctor had his college scholarship terminated. The NAACP Youth Council renewed picketing in 1963 under the leadership of Elnora Adams. The theaters finally agreed to desegregate in the summer of 1963.

SANITATION STRIKE OF 1968

The struggle that received the most public attention was the sanitation workers' strike of 1968. Some might argue that this was a labor event rather than a civil rights action. But it was very much a part of the local civil rights struggle in the sense that it spoke to the fundamental issue of income inequality between whites and blacks generally. The sanitation strike of 1968 was preceded by two previous strikes, one in 1964 and one in 1966, both of which were settled within a short time. In the 1966 strike, City Manager Lynn Andrews fired 70 percent of the Sanitation Department's workforce, but they were later reinstated. Strikers were represented by black attorneys James B. Sanderlin and Frank Peterman.

In 1968, there were several nationally significant sanitation strikes, including those in New York City, Memphis and nearby Tampa. Martin Luther King Jr., president of the Southern Christian Leadership Conference (SCLC), was in Memphis supporting the black sanitation workers' strike there when he was assassinated on April 4, 1968. About one month later, sanitation workers went on strike in St. Petersburg. A new pay plan had gone into effect that reduced pay for sanitation workers from $101.40 for six days' work to $73.00 for five days' work. This amounted to a reduction of 15 percent per hour and 28 percent per week's pay. The new pay program was initially presented as a month-long trial, after which savings realized would be shared with the workers. This did not happen. The workers then went on strike. Local attorney Jim Sanderlin again represented the strikers. He and strike leader Joe Savage negotiated for a $0.25-per-hour increase. Andrews countered with $0.05 and offered to rescind the new pay plan and revert to the previous plan. The strikers voted to hold out for a $0.20-per-hour increase. City Manager Andrews responded by refusing to negotiate further and fired 52 workers, soon to be followed by the firing of another 150 workers.

On May 23, attorney Ike Williams, president of the NAACP, came to the support of the strikers by calling for a "selective buying" campaign—a boycott of white-owned businesses. Also, Mayor Don Jones broke ranks with the city council, criticizing the city manager and charging the city with "sowing the seeds of the present garbage crisis." At this point, a number of fires were set, causing damage to a lumberyard, automobiles and one house—some targeting nonstrikers. Who set the fires is unknown. The strikers disavowed the fires, and Sanderlin and Savage formed an Anti-Violence Committee.

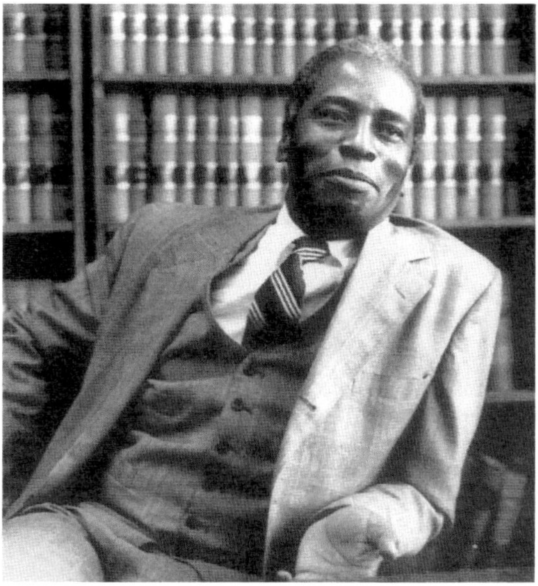

Attorney James B. Sanderlin was prominent in seeking open accommodations for black Major League Baseball players, representing city sanitation workers in the 1968 strike and in the desegregation of public schools. He later became a county and circuit court judge. Sanderlin Middle School in south St. Petersburg is named in his honor.

On June 7, the first of some forty sanitation worker marches took place starting on Twenty-Second Street near Jordan School and ending at city hall. Martin Luther King's brother, A.D. King, agreed to support the strike and participated in a march. While the march was peaceful, it was conducted without a permit, and police arrested 43 protestors, many of whom blocked traffic. King continued to support the march, and Reverend Ralph Abernathy spoke to more than 1,000 people at Gibbs High School on July 31. On August 14, local civil rights activist Joe Waller (who later took the name Omali Yeshitela) was arrested by police for misdemeanors including simple assault on a police officer (he was later convicted). He stated that after his arrest he was subjected to police brutality, which police denied. The *Times* interviewed persons who stated that photographs showing injuries were circulated in the black community after his release.

Two years earlier, Waller had ripped a racially offensive painting from the walls of city hall after pleas by other black community leaders to remove it were refused. He was sentenced to three years in prison for this offense, and he had served eighteen months when Circuit Judge David Seth Walker reduced his sentence to time served in 1973. Judge Walker stated that the offense could not be excused but that he understood Waller's indignation. Later, Judge Walker noted that a similar act committed in 2000 would likely lead to probation or the withholding of a formal finding of guilt. In 1998, the city council considered

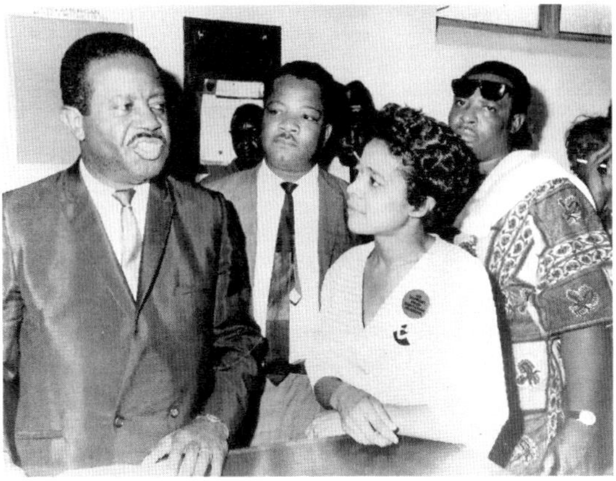

Left: Reverend Ralph Abernathy (left) and A.D. King (center), brother of Martin Luther King Jr., came to St. Petersburg to support the sanitation workers' strike, 1968. *Courtesy St. Petersburg Museum of History.*

Below: Sanitation workers march on city hall. Joseph Savage (front right) was the strike leader, and James Sanderlin (left of Savage) was attorney for the striking workers, image 1968. From *Tampa Bay Times*.

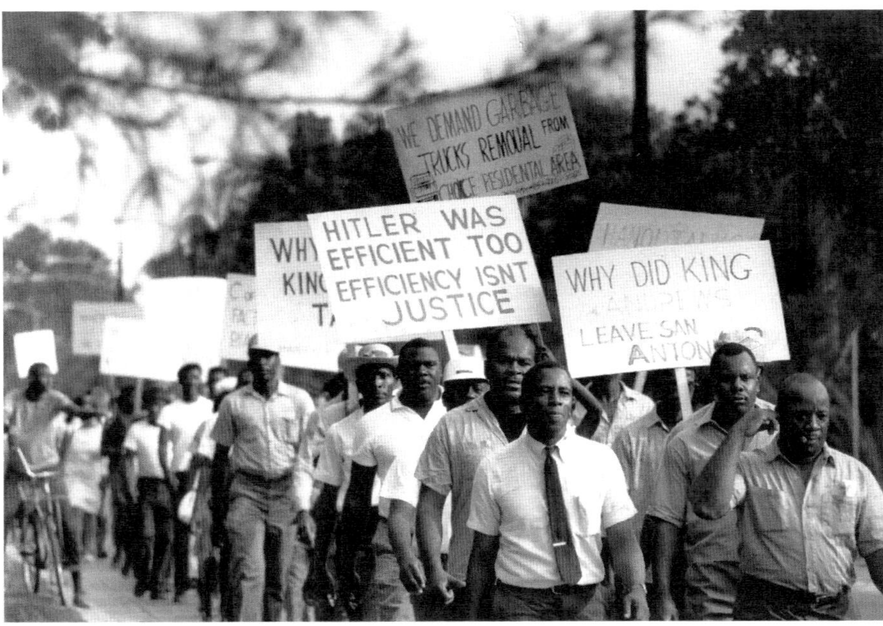

awarding Waller with a laudatory plaque as a form of apology for the pain and suffering he incurred as a result of ripping down the painting but became locked on the issue in a tie vote. Ultimately, he was granted clemency by the governor and cabinet, enabling him to have his voting rights restored.

On August 15, 1968, the city council passed an ordinance against impeding public travel on streets and sidewalks. The strikers had begun using sidewalks for marches rather than obtaining permits for marches on the streets. On August 17, civil violence erupted in the area of the city now known as Midtown. The strike leadership denounced the violence. Some 350 National Guardsmen were activated to support local police. By the next day, there were fifty-nine arrests, eleven arsons and an estimated $120,000 in property damage. The number of arsons later rose to thirty-four, and property damage increased to between $350,000 and $400,000. Reverend Enoch Davis, writing in 1979, declared "the burnings and lootings were among the most devastating experiences ever to take place" in the city. NAACP president Ike Williams stated that the arrest of Joe Waller and the ordinances against impeding public travel, perceived as targeting the sanitation strike marches, precipitated the violence.

About two months before this civil violence, a group of "Concerned Clergy" met with the city council to try to mediate the crisis. One issue raised was offensive language still remaining in the city charter calling for residential segregation and the holding of all-white primary elections. The council agreed to rescind those provisions. Also, a few days before the violence, Mayor Don Jones initiated the Community Alliance in cooperation with the St. Petersburg Chamber of Commerce. The Community Alliance was a biracial organization whose mission was to address poor job opportunities for blacks, renovate slum housing and expand and improve educational opportunities. But these efforts came too late to prevent violence.

On August 30, after 116 days, the strike was finally settled after great personal sacrifice by the workers involved and their families. Sanitation workers who had been fired and wished to return to their jobs were rehired. The new pay and work plan was rescinded. Sanitation collectors soon received an eight-cent-per-hour pay raise.

Mayor Don Jones later stated that the strike allowed St. Petersburg to "grow up and become a part of the twentieth century and part of the United States." Anthropologist Evelyn Newman Phillips called the sanitation strike a watershed in the history of St. Petersburg. The protest led the city to open black input into city decision-making. A voting district composed primarily of African Americans was soon established. In 1969, C. Bette Wimbish became the first black to be elected to the city council and then to serve as vice-chair. She later served as Florida deputy secretary of commerce.

INTEGRATION OF SCHOOLS

Historically, black schoolteachers in St. Petersburg were paid significantly less than their white counterparts until a suit forced equal pay in 1945. Black schools were notorious for being poorly maintained and equipped, usually getting hand-me-down books. Despite the U.S. Supreme Court's 1954 *Brown v. Board of Education* ruling declaring segregated schools illegal, between 1954 and 1963 nine new black schools were opened in Pinellas. Rather than integrate St. Petersburg Jr. College, a new all-black Gibbs Jr. College was opened in 1957. Ten years after the *Brown* decision, only 2 percent of Pinellas's black students attended school with whites.

The State of Florida and the Pinellas School Board managed to effectively delay local application of the *Brown* decision until 1964. As early as 1960, educator C. Bette Wimbish ran for the school board in order to try to change the system from within. She was the first black person to run for countywide elected office. While she did not win, she received more than ten thousand votes, 70 percent of them coming from whites. In 1964, attorney Jim Sanderlin, with support of Dr. Ralph Wimbish and the NAACP, took on the cause of desegregating local schools. In that year, Leon Bradley Sr., a black Clearwater police officer and vice-president of the Clearwater NAACP, decided to challenge the school board's obstructionist policies. Specifically, Bradley wanted to transfer his son from the all-black Pinellas High School to John F. Kennedy Middle School, which was less crowded and better equipped. He wanted his son to have a better education. The NAACP Legal Defense Fund contacted the St. Petersburg law firm of White, Peterman and Sanderlin to represent Bradley. It filed suit on January 15, 1965, and won. Federal District Judge Joseph Lieb called for a "comprehensive" desegregation plan that "eliminated dual attendance zones and reassigned pupils, faculty, and other personnel on a non-racial basis."

The school board attorney and Frank White's associate, Jim Sanderlin, developed a plan for desegregation to be accomplished by school year 1968–69. Unfortunately, the plan had two major flaws. Firstly, the definition of a "desegregated school" was vague and allowed school board officials to legally declare a school integrated even if it had just one black student. Consequently, in 1967, the school board claimed that all twelve of the county's high schools were desegregated. But Boca Ciega had one black student, Gibbs had one white student, Northeast had one black teacher but no black students and Clearwater's Pinellas High remained all black. Secondly, the plan called for the closing of black schools, which would greatly hurt the black community economically and socially.

Additional court orders were issued in 1970 and 1971 seeking to fix the loopholes and flaws in the 1965 plan and fully realize an integrated school system. These rulings affected Hillsborough and Sarasota Counties, as well as Pinellas. Finally, again facing a court order, the school board voluntarily agreed to implement a comprehensive busing plan to achieve integration without closing black schools. As an example under this plan, Gibbs High School, previously nearly all black, became 70 percent white. No school had more than 30 percent black students. Busing zones changed regularly so that no white elementary students were bused for more than two years. Black students were bused constantly as there were not enough black students to meet racial quotas in all schools. All schools throughout St. Petersburg and Pinellas County finally became integrated on this basis, seventeen years after the U.S. Supreme Court first ruled segregated schools unconstitutional. Even so, Pinellas County was the first county to integrate its schools in Florida.

While many in the black community celebrated the advantages of integration and a more open society, this did not come without a price. Some mourned the loss of predominantly black schools and the community cultures and social networks built up around them. Some black students, previously sheltered by these cultures and networks, actually had their first experience with overt racist hostility in the newly integrated schools. While all schools now had black students, many lacked black administrators who also served as role models. An exception was St. Petersburg High School, where black educator Vyrle Davis was appointed principal in 1973. But in 1980, eleven of thirty-three middle and high schools still did not have black administrators. The percentage of black teachers was also below the affirmative action goal.

Jim Sanderlin went on to become the first black person to be elected countywide when he was elected judge in 1972. In 1985, he was appointed circuit judge. He died in 1990. A school is named in his honor in South St. Pete.

Throughout all these events, various mediating groups were formed to try to improve conditions. They were called Bi-Racial Committees, Community Relations Commissions and the Community Alliance. Also of great significance was the voluntarily organized Ambassadors Club. While much has improved, like other communities, there is still work to be done. We no longer focus only on racism, discrimination and prejudice as it affects African Americans but now address all forms of prejudice and discrimination, whether that be against persons of particular ethnic groups such as Latinos; based on gender, different sexual orientation or age; or against the disabled, persons who are poor, persons who are of a different faith or others.

The city council recently called for the establishment of a new citizens group, named St. Pete Together, to address racism, prejudice and equal opportunity. The group developed the following vision and mission statement:

> *Our mission is to reach into every corner of our city and seek those who like us, demand civility, respect, and inclusivity. Together, we become a powerful voice and catalyst to address all issues of social justice. We will: educate, deliberate and create opportunities for an inclusive prosperity; advocate against racism, prejudice, and discrimination; encourage dialogue and cultivate a community steeped in the celebration of diversity based upon respect and appreciation for the worth and dignity of all persons.*

CIVIL RIGHTS BENCHMARKS

1954	Supreme Court issues *Brown v. Board of Education, Topeka, Kansas*.
1957	Civil Rights Act enacted prohibiting intimidating, coercing or otherwise interfering with the right of persons to vote for president and members of Congress.
1960	Civil Rights Act enacted providing for federal inspections of voter registration rolls and establishing penalties for obstruction of a person's attempt to register to vote or to vote.
	President Eisenhower deploys troops in Little Rock, Arkansas, to safeguard the integration of a high school.
	Four black students conduct a sit-in at a North Carolina lunch counter.
1961	Supreme Court in *Boynton v. Virginia* bans segregation in terminals for interstate bus transportation.

1963	March on Washington for Jobs and Freedom takes place. Martin Luther King Jr. gives his "I Have a Dream" speech at the Lincoln Memorial.
	President Kennedy is assassinated, November 22.
1964	Civil Rights Act enacted outlawing major forms of segregation, unequal application of voter registration requirements and racial segregation in schools.
1965	Voters Rights Act enacted prohibiting states from imposing voting procedures, such as literacy tests, that deny or abridge the right of a citizen to vote on account of race or color; also required is preclearance with the federal government by jurisdictions with a history of discriminatory voting practices.
1968	Martin Luther King Jr. is assassinated, April 4.
	Robert F. Kennedy is assassinated, June 5.
	Fifth Circuit of Appeals rules that Florida and six other states must integrate all remaining black schools or shut them down.
1969	Supreme Court in *Alexander v. Holmes County Board of Education* orders all school districts to terminate "dual school" systems at once and operate only "unitary schools."
1970	Supreme Court in *Swann v. Charlotte-Mecklenberg Board of Education* approves use of busing to achieve integration.

Resources used in this chapter include Raymond Arsenault, *St. Petersburg and the Florida Dream* and *Freedom Riders: 1961 and the Struggle for Racial Justice*; City of St. Petersburg, "Staff Report on Jennie Hall Pool Landmark Designation Request (HPC 11-90300001)"; Anita Cutting, "From Joe Waller to Omali Yeshitela: How a Controversial Mural Changed a Man," honors thesis, USF; Enoch Davis, *On the Bethel Trail*; Junius English, "Black Power Still Lives!: The Uhuru Movement in Saint Petersburg, Florida (1971–2001)," thesis, Florida A&M; Peyton L. Jones, "Struggle in the Sunshine City: The Movement for Racial Equality in St. Petersburg, FL, 1955–1968," thesis, University of South Florida; Will Michaels, "Civil Rights in St. Pete," *Northeast Journal*, 2012; Darryl Paulson and Janet Stiff, "An Empty Victory: The St. Petersburg Sanitation Strike, 1968," *Florida Historical Quarterly*; John Howard McNeilly, *The St. Petersburg Sanitation Strike of 1968: A Process in Political Empowerment*; Rosalie Peck and Jon Wilson, *St. Petersburg's Historic 22nd Street South*; Evelyn Newman Phillips, "An Ethnohistorical Analysis of the Political Economy of Ethnicity Among African Americans in St. Petersburg, Florida," dissertation, University of South Florida; Sandra W. Rooks, *Black America Series: St. Petersburg, FL*; *St. Petersburg Times* (various); James A. Schnur, "Desegregation of Public Schools in Pinellas County, Florida"; School Board of Pinellas County, *A Tradition of Excellence, Pinellas County Schools: 1912–1987*; *Weekly Challenger* (February 24, 2011); and Jon L. Wilson, "Shaping the Dream: A Survey of Post World War II St. Petersburg, 1946–1963," thesis, University of South Florida.

St. Petersburg

A Sense of Place

Defining St. Petersburg's sense of place, or unique identity, is challenging. There is much data to consider and analyze. There is also the question of identity as perceived by whom? Depending on one's perspective—perceived identity will vary from person to person and group to group. The perspective of a resident is different from the perspective of a visitor. Here is the author's perspective, as a forty-year resident and someone active in social services, neighborhood activities, museums and historic preservation.

Subtropical Paradise

Perhaps the foremost aspect of our sense of place or unique identity is our warm semitropical climate and land surrounded by water. We all laugh about how in 1885, Dr. W.C. Van Bibber delivered a paper to the American Medical Association meeting in New Orleans entitled "Peninsular and Sub-Peninsular Air and Climates." In his paper, he declared the lower Pinellas Peninsula as the ideal place for a "health city" that would maximize health and longevity. Van Bibber's paper influenced Hamilton Disston to select today's nearby Gulfport as the site for his visionary metropolis. The paper was widely circulated by the Orange Belt Railway to attract tourists, and medical publisher and St. Petersburg pioneer F.A. Davis did the same through his vast national medical publishing network.

From the very beginning, St. Petersburg invented the idea of selling the city's most plentiful commodity, sunshine, to tourists and prospective new residents. Along with sunshine came access to the bay and Gulf. In the early years of our history, one did not need to be rich to buy waterfront property, and those who did not have waterfront property had access to the downtown Waterfront Parks and pier area or the many other waterfront parks and water bodies about the city. Our plentiful fishing not only offered recreation but also helped us get through the tough times of the Great Depression and World War II. Our blue skies are often filled with billowy white cumulus clouds. St. Petersburg's clouds are its mountains. And then there are the brilliant sunrises and sunsets, their colorful reflections shimmering on the waters.

Famously, the *Evening Independent*, dating from the days when we had two newspapers, gave the paper away free if the sun did not shine at least some time during the day. Over the course of seventy-five years of publishing, the city averaged fewer than five days a year without sun. We hold the Guinness World Record for the most consecutive days of sunshine—768 days that began in 1967. The average winter temperature is seventy-two degrees. We were dubbed the "Sunshine City" in 1910, and the moniker still holds today.

The city's greatest asset is its downtown Waterfront Parks, including the pier. The fifteen downtown Waterfront Parks, starting on the south with Poynter Park and ending on the north with Coffee Pot Park, encompass more than 100 acres and stretch along the Bay for more than four miles. St. Petersburg has one of the largest Waterfront Park systems in the nation. Other parks include Abercrombie, Maximo, Boyd Hill Nature Preserve and Weedon Island. There is also the Downtown Public Marina, the largest city marina in Florida. Overall, St. Petersburg has 125 parks covering more than 2,300 acres, or nearly 9 percent of its land mass. The city's waterfront parks and pier serve as important recreational and social centers.

From the very start, parkland has been a city highlight. City founder John C. Williams Sr. set aside a downtown city block for a park that served as the town square for many years. After his death, it was named for him. This was followed, after a fierce struggle, with the preservation of the downtown waterfront for parkland, the Waterfront Parks. These were added to over the years, most recently with the addition of Albert Whitted Park. Mayor Baker's program to establish parks within one mile of every residence furthered this tradition. Nearby beaches such as Fort De Soto and Caladesi are frequently identified as among the world's best. Parks and beaches went hand in hand with the early boosting of St. Petersburg as a healthful city, the sunshine city, an exotic subtropical place to visit if not live in.

St. Petersburg is also promoted as a "City of Trees." For twenty years, the city has received the Tree City USA Award. Since 2001, some eighteen thousand trees have been planted. In addition to the traditional oaks and a wide variety of palms, there are the Royal Poinciana, Gold Trees, Jacarandas and Kapoks and Banyans. A variety of Bougainvillea sprinkle the city. The sweeping, yellow spans of the Skyway Bridge offer an amazing visual introduction to our city and its surrounding waters when approaching from the south. It is the longest cable suspension bridge in the Western Hemisphere and is another of the city's striking visual symbols. Smaller bridges offer their charms as well—the Snell Isle Venetian Bridge positioned on the scenic Coffee Pot Boulevard and "Thrill Hill" passing over Salt Creek on Third Street South in Old Southeast. Thrill Hill is named for the brief rollercoaster sensation it gives as you drive over it.

At one time, St. Pete was known as the "City of Green Benches." This is a tradition and image that the city tried to wipe away. Ironically, the green benches were originally part and parcel of St. Petersburg's emphasis on sunshine, outdoor living and friendliness. At one time, there were more than three thousand public green benches mostly in the downtown area. Today, there are about four hundred, mostly in the parks. Maria Vesperi in her classic book *City of Green Benches* stated that the benches "symbolized [for the elderly] welcome, friendliness, and, most of all acceptance." Their removal destroyed a place where social support among the elderly could be found and sent a message that seniors were no longer welcome, their important economic contribution made to the city over many years no longer appreciated.

Since removal of the green benches in the 1960s, the city's demographic profile has changed. In 1960, the median age of our city was a fraction over 47, and the percent of persons 65 years of age or more was 28 percent—this actually peaked at 31 percent in 1970. As of 2000, the proportion of persons 65 years of age and over had dropped to a little over 17 percent, and the mean age had dropped to 39.3. St. Petersburg's dense senior population did not really begin to materialize until 1950. Between 1930 and 1940, the proportion of persons 65 or older ranged between 10 and 15 percent, although this was also substantially higher than the U.S. population.

Are we at a point of maturity where we can put the green benches back? Hopefully the present character of our city is one where persons of all

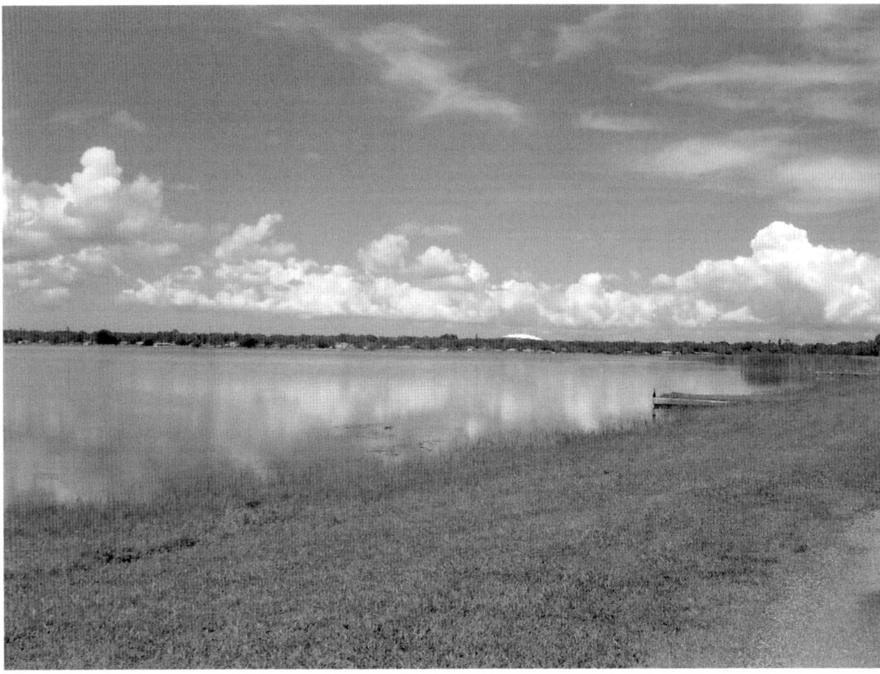

Lake Maggiore in South St. Petersburg, looking north toward Tropicana Field. The lake covers 385 acres and is surrounded on the south by Boyd Hill Nature Preserve, on the north by Del Holmes Park and Lake Maggiore Shores Neighborhood and on the east by Lake Maggiore Park. Lake Maggiore was originally named Aguada de San Francisco by the Spanish and was later known simply as Salt Lake, probably because for most of its history it was a saltwater estuary of the bay.

ages and all walks of life are appreciated and welcomed. This is a stated aspiration in the city's Vision 2020 document, and it is repeated in the city's Comprehensive Plan: "All races and cultures will be celebrated, enjoying their diversity, and participating and claiming ownership in the process of building community. All citizens shall have an equal opportunity to enjoy the physical, social, and economic benefits of St. Petersburg."

Such institutions as the Community Alliance and, most recently, St. Pete Together were created to help achieve this. The city established an Office on Aging in 1973 to further address the social and health needs of seniors. Pinellas County and St. Petersburg have also long embraced their children, especially those in need. Since 1946, a special taxing district called the Juvenile Welfare Board (JWB) has provided funding and technical support for children's services. Six times the city has been designated one of the 100 Best Communities for Young People by the America's Promise Alliance. Also to be celebrated is the city's fifty-year Sister City partnership with Takamatsu, Japan. Annual delegation, teacher and student exchanges have helped to build mutual understanding and goodwill between two unique cultures. The St. Petersburg International Folk Festival Society (SPIFFS), representing more than thirty ethic groups, has done much to build intercultural appreciation. Its annual festival event is always a highlight.

One characteristic that has improved over the years is the city's protection of its green space and bird life. We have always had our environmental champions, the most celebrated of whom was Katherine Bell Tippetts. While they did establish nature preserves and accomplished other measures to protect our environment, they were up against runaway development, perhaps most notably the dredging of the 1950s and '60s. State regulation, perhaps more so than local, has since added substantial protection. In 2008, St. Petersburg became the first designated Green City in the United States. In 2001, the city held a series of workshops and other activities involving several hundred people that resulted in a vision statement for the year 2020, commonly known as Vision 2020. This led to the city-revised Comprehensive Plan and new Land Development Regulations (LDRs) enacted in 2007. The city's Comprehensive Plan states that "St. Petersburg is a unique and special place. It is blessed with geography between the Gulf of Mexico and Tampa Bay that provides a natural setting matched by few waterfront cities anywhere in the world." Cities are made and shaped by their geography and climate, as well as by their people.

DISTINCTIVE ARCHITECTURE

Vision 2020 plainly states the challenge for our city's built environment: "Cities over time grow, develop and evolve into different places. All too often, the unique character of towns and cities is replaced by mass-produced, cookie-cutter neighborhoods, strip centers, malls and buildings which are not designed to reinforce the local context. Many cities have lost their identity, becoming known as 'Anywhere, USA' and offering little stimulus to the souls of residents."

In 2006, the city held a Mayor's Historic Preservation Summit during which a presentation was made on the "Historic Character of St. Petersburg." This presentation identified the city's unique architecture as one outstanding city feature, including historic buildings such as the open-air post office, the

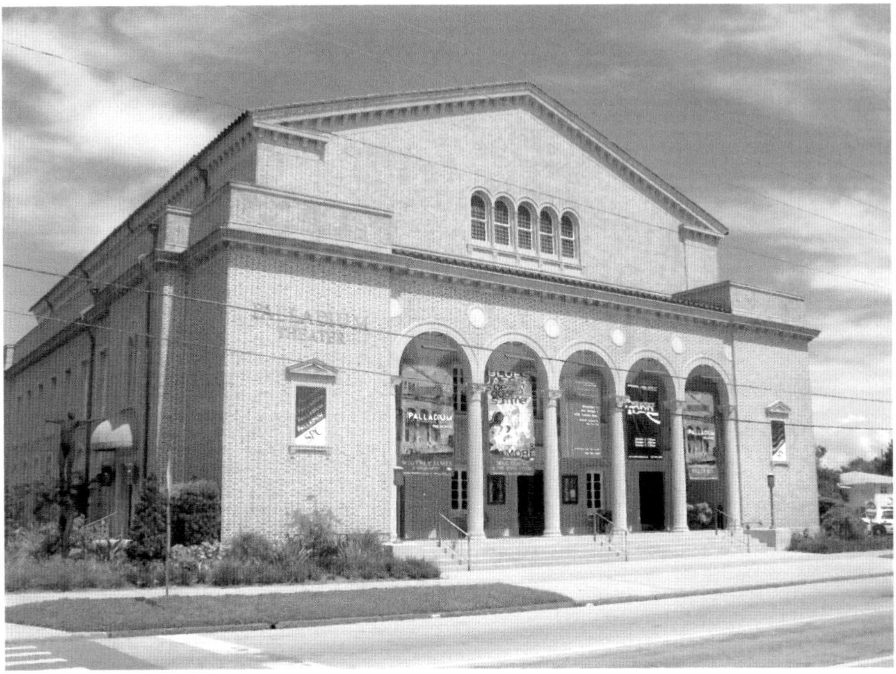

Another great historic preservation accomplishment is the Palladium Theater, which was designated as a historic landmark by the city and St. Petersburg College in 2012. The building was originally the First Church of Christ, Science. It was built in the Italian Renaissance style in 1925.

Vinoy Hotel, city hall, the Snell Arcade and the Inverted Pyramid Pier building. The Jungle Prada on the west side was also cited. A distinctive architectural style—some might call it the signature style of the city, especially in the downtown—is Mediterranean Revival. Borrowed from the sunny Mediterranean, these buildings are typically asymmetrical in plan and one or two stories when found in homes, with a vertical feature such as a chimney or square tower, as well as a roof of terra-cotta tile. These homes and other buildings were often known as "Spanish castles," fairy tale–like buildings with grillwork and various decorative features. One outstanding example of this architecture is the Snell Arcade, the towers of which are used by Saint Petersburg Presentation for its logo. Another splendid example is the Vinoy. In many respects, this style of architecture is a good fit for what St. Petersburg was all about historically and, to a large degree, remains. It fit well with a city surrounded by water hyping health, sunshine, outdoor recreation and the exotic.

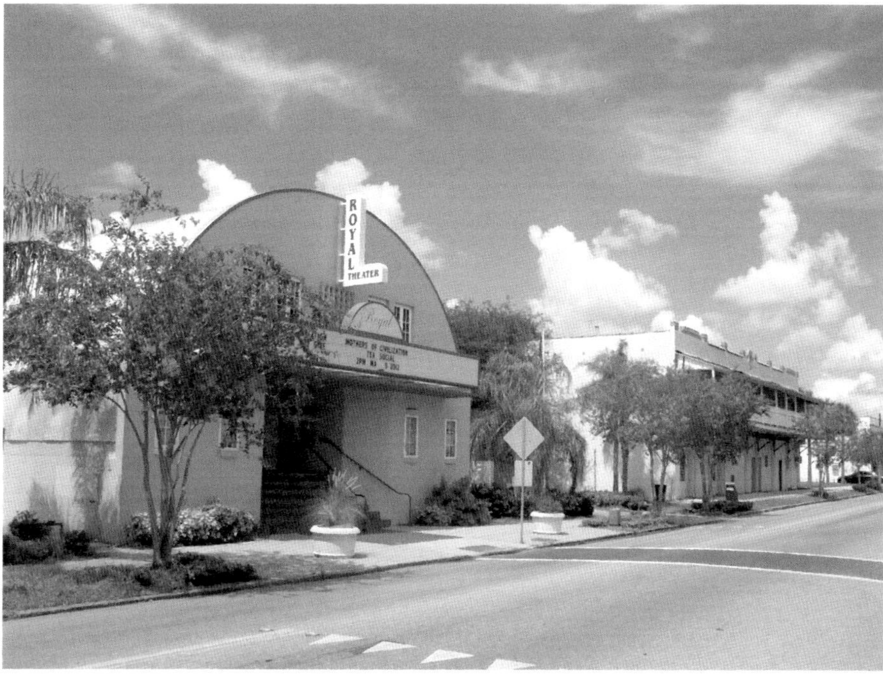

The Royal Theater on the historic "Deuces" (Twenty-second Street South) in Midtown. The Royal Theater was built from a Quonset hut, which is unusual in St. Petersburg. The Royal opened in 1948 and was one of two theaters to exclusively serve the African American community during the era of segregation. Since the theater's closing in about 1967, it has served as an important youth center for the African American community and is currently operated by the Boys and Girls Club of the Suncoast as a cultural arts center.

There is, of course, an exciting assortment of architectural styles throughout the city in addition to Mediterranean Revival. Our city's grand hotels especially reflect a range of architectural styles. There are also our churches. St. Petersburg was once known as a "City of Churches." Several churches have been designated local landmarks, including Bethel African Methodist Episcopal (Gothic Revival), First Baptist (Neoclassical), St. Peter's Cathedral (Florida Gothic) and, very recently, First Church of Christ, Scientist, now known as the Palladium Theater (Italian Renaissance Revival). Each building has its story to tell. A city's history is written on its buildings.

As might be expected at a Historic Preservation Summit, no contemporary buildings were featured. But certainly newer buildings need to be considered in regard to our current sense of place. Our downtown, sometimes called "Everybody's Neighborhood," has seen the increasing presence of high-

St. Petersburg's downtown has become a mixture of the new and the historic. Seen here is the modern twenty-nine-story "400 Beach" (named after its address), built in 2007 by Opus and located not far from the historic Mediterranean Revival–style Vinoy Renaissance Hotel built in 1925. The restoration of the Vinoy in 1992 is largely credited with revitalizing St. Petersburg's downtown.

rise buildings: Bayfront Tower, the Plaza, the Tower at One Progress Plaza (formerly the Bank of America Tower), the Florencia, the Cloisters, Signature Place, Ovation, Parkshore Plaza, the Progress Energy Building and 400 Beach Drive. Also there is BayWalk, the recently renovated Mahaffey and the new Dali Museum, with its unique boulder-studded landscaping.

Many of these buildings are changing our identity from a downtown with a strong 1920s feel to a mix of the traditional and the modern—a community that is seeking to preserve the best of the historic and traditional and at the same time add to it a new dimension in architecture and efficient use of space. Three of the tower buildings (the Florencia, the Cloisters and Parkshore Plaza) and also BayWalk carry forth at least some elements of the Mediterranean Revival style. Others are of International or Modern style. It has been said that beauty is not just copying someone else—beauty has to come from within. The challenge of today's and tomorrow's architecture in St. Petersburg, particularly for public buildings, is to find or create styles that reflect the spirit of our community. As stated in Vision 2020, architecture that is generic and lacks connection to our city's unique sense of place should be avoided.

Strong Neighborhoods

The 2006 "Historic Character" Presentation also identified the variety of our neighborhoods as a unique city attribute. The distinct architectural styles and unique landscape elements such as granite curbs, brick streets, mature vegetation, hex blocks and, in some cases, alley systems were noted. Also emphasized were the many strong, organized neighborhood associations supporting these neighborhoods and our city as a whole. There are 110 neighborhood associations of record, although not all are active. Many of our mayors and city council persons have been active in their neighborhood associations and the Council of Neighborhood Associations (CONA), some serving as association presidents. In many respects, the neighborhood associations have served as training grounds for future city officials. The same may be said of the St. Petersburg Chamber of Commerce . These institutions are strong voices in city policy making. They both offer strong leadership development programs. The unique role played by neighborhoods is also recognized in Vision 2020 and protected in the new Land Development Regulations (LDRs). Vision 2020 states that neighborhoods "shall be the basic building block for social equality and shared enjoyment of St. Petersburg's unique quality of life" and that the city should "[p]rotect and reinforce the unique character of each neighborhood."

"Big Town Feel"

St. Petersburg, with a current city-estimated population of about 255,000 people, is the seventy-seventh-largest city in the nation. It ranks above Jersey City, Orlando, Birmingham and Richmond. It is the fourth-largest city in Florida after Jacksonville, Miami and Tampa. St. Petersburg also covers an area of about sixty-one square miles (not counting lakes and other bodies of water within the city limits—another seventy-three square miles).

The structure of a town can facilitate meaningful connections between people. For those living in the downtown area, now about seven thousand people, it's possible to walk to markets, shops, restaurants and entertainment. Not only do people see one another at a neighborhood association meeting, but they also connect at these other venues. Aside from the downtown, most neighborhoods do not offer a mix of residential, commercial and culture, other than recreation, within walking distance. Vision 2020 gives some acknowledgement to this: "Neighborhoods need to contain limited neighborhood friendly commerce serving the basic needs of the neighborhood." The Comprehensive Plan speaks of downtown as an "urban village."

Not feeling crowded or closed in gives us the feeling of a city smaller than it actually is. St. Pete's general profile is flat. The original town plat unknowingly facilitated this. City founders John C. Williams and Peter Demens, copying Hamilton Disston's unrealized plans for what is now Gulfport, provided for a city with streets one hundred feet wide—they were planning for a grand city. This street structure also helped spread out city development, keeping a more open, small-city, pedestrian-friendly feel. The new land development regulations seek to reinforce the feel of a low-profile city even at the foot of new high-rises through use of long setback requirements. Also, the Beach Drive high-rise towers have a mandated minimum distance between them, causing them to be spaced out.

St. Petersburg architect Tim Clemmons described our community as having a "big town feel," a city with an open social, economic and political scene—a community relatively accepting of new people into the system. Some say that the charm of St. Petersburg is its mix of town-like and cosmopolitan charms. This is particularly true of downtown—see the historic Detroit Hotel across the street from the Bank of America Tower. But also it is this greater opportunity to connect with other people because of the ability to walk to stores, restaurants and parks.

Tourism and Other Sectors of Our Economy

Tourism is still an important sector of the economy in St. Pete, and the community is still largely known for tourism along with all that goes with it—sunshine, outdoor recreation, beaches, boating, fishing, hotels and motels, restaurants and more. According to city government, about 9 million visitors come to the city annually. Countywide tourism generates $6.1 billion per year. Vision 2020 credits tourism with creating a legacy of parks and recreational facilities, cultural activities, museums, hotels, restaurants and shops that "provide a unique quality of life."

This is true in large part, although certainly some of this would have occurred without tourism. C. Perry Snell probably saw the Waterfront Parks as benefiting sales in his nearby residential developments as much as benefiting tourism. It is estimated that the Rays baseball team attendance includes 455,000 people per year from out of area. Recently tourism, while still important, has been superseded in economic impact by the financial and medical sectors of our economy. All Children's Hospital is one of the best children's hospitals in the state and recently became part of the Johns Hopkins Health System. Marine and environmental science has also become an important sector, with an impact of $250 million countywide. This sector thrives because of our ready access to water and marine life, as well as research support from area colleges and universities. Retail sales and real estate also have their importance. Tyrone Mall was the largest shopping mall in the Bay area when it opened in 1972, and it still remains the largest in St. Petersburg.

St. Petersburg is also known for its rich assortment of community events, attracting tourists and locals alike. These include Ribfest, Bluegrass Festival, American Stage in the Park, Saturday Morning Market, First Friday, Festival of the States, the Honda Grand Prix, Circus McGurkus, Art Arbor and cultural and educational institutions such the Arts Center, museums and galleries, sporting events, schools, colleges, universities and libraries. The city has recently sought to brand itself as the "City of Museums" and a "Cultural Center for Florida." The Florida Orchestra, which performs at the Mahaffey Theater, is one of the leading professional symphony orchestras in Florida. The Dali (serving 370,000 visitors annually), the Morean Arts Center Chihuly Glass Art Collection and the Museum of Fine Arts on Beach Drive also stand out. The Museum of Fine Arts offers an outstanding collection of works by Cézanne, Rodin, Gauguin, Renoir and Monet. The museum building itself is a work of art designed by John Volk in the Palladian style. Not to be forgotten are the St. Petersburg Museum of History on the approach to the pier, the Holocaust Museum and the Dr. Carter G. Woodson African American Museum near "the Deuces" (Twenty-second Street) in Midtown. The city's website lists "50 Fabulous Things to Do in St. Petersburg."

This "fun in the sun" tourism identity does have its challenge: an economic sector that is difficult to compete in and provides lower-paying jobs. In recent years, the city has been aggressive in seeking to diversify the economy and upgrade the quality of jobs and compensation. The city offers eight different incentive programs to try to attract more new and expanded downtown businesses, such as Enterprise Zone incentives. The Bayboro Marine Science District is the largest such marine science cluster in the Southeast (the Stanford Research Institute, or SRI; Marine Technology Research Center; National Oceanic & Atmospheric Administration, NOAA; Fisheries Service Southeast Regional Office; and University of South Florida College of Marine Science, among others).

City government identifies six major business clusters: medical technologies and services; information technologies; marine sciences; financial services; manufacturing; and arts, culture and tourism. Also, historic preservation adds to our economic vitality. It increases property values, creates construction jobs, provides affordable housing and affordable venues for small businesses, makes possible heritage tourism and adds to overall quality of life—an important consideration in attracting new residents and employers.

OUR PEOPLE

Sense of place is not limited to climate, geography and the built environment but also includes the people living there. As Shakespeare wrote, "What is a city but the people?" While people make and build a city, they themselves are a vital part of it. What are the unique characteristics of our city's people? One characteristic that comes to mind are the dreamers. Both historians Ray Arsenault and Gary Mormino have used the word "dream" in their respective works on St. Petersburg and Florida—referring to St. Petersburg's "continuing effort to create a subtropical dreamland" and to a state that "imported dreamers and exported oranges." Dreamers make up an important part of St. Petersburg's uniqueness. To name just a few, there were John and Sarah Williams and Peter Demens, who emigrated from Detroit and Russia to found their subtropical dreamland. There was William L. Straub, who emigrated from North Dakota to find a more healthful climate and become a leader in creating his dreamland, most notably his role in establishing the Waterfront Parks, although that was certainly

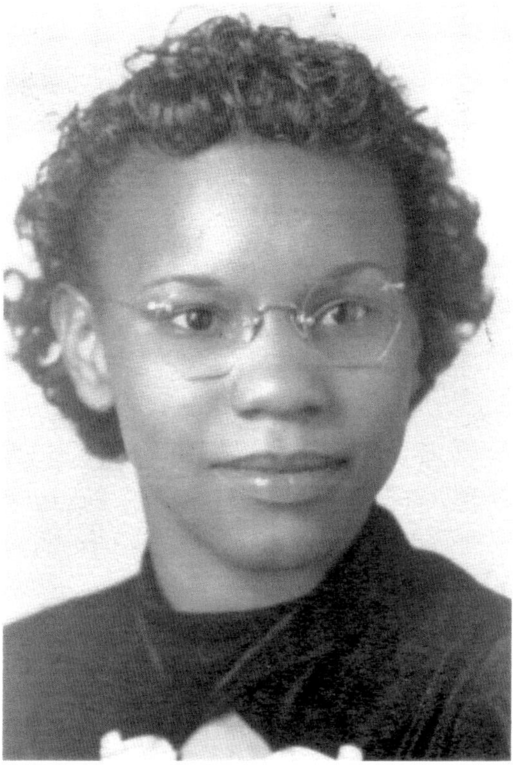

Johnnie Ruth Clarke was the first African American to receive a doctorate from the University of Florida and was a leading city educator. She fostered medical programs and championed health issues benefiting the poor. The Johnnie Ruth Clarke Center on the site of the former Mercy Hospital was named in her honor, image circa 1940. *Courtesy St. Petersburg Museum of History.*

not his only accomplishment. Straub's ability to find win-win solutions and middle ground serves as a model for civic responsibility to this day.

There were the exuberant personalities and visionaries of the Roaring Twenties, such as Noel Mitchell, Katherine Bell Tippetts, John Lodwick, Elder Jordan Sr., Babe Ruth and others. There were the civil rights leaders of the 1950s and '60s. The builders of our downtown high-rises were dreamers. In modern times, our dreamers have included such people as actress Angela Bassett; Olympic gold medalist Nicole Haislett, who trained at North Shore Pool; light middleweight boxing champion Winky Wright; singer and actor Patrick Wilson; Alvin Ailey dancer Briana Reed; and Daniel Ulbricht, now with the New York City Ballet.

Educator Johnnie Ruth Clarke did not immigrate to St. Petersburg. She was born here. She said that she "came from rock bottom." Pulling herself up by her bootstraps, she became one of our city's leading educators. She was the first African American to receive a doctorate from the University of Florida. Eventually serving as associate dean of what is now St. Petersburg College, she fostered medical programs and championed health issues benefiting the poor. The Johnnie Ruth Clarke Health Center on the site of the former Mercy Hospital in Midtown was named for her. "Blacks and whites have built this town and sustained it," she once said. "That's what I like about my hometown; the people 'get it together.'" These and countless other dreamers are perhaps what is most unique about St. Petersburg. True, there are dreamers in other cities too, but these are our unique dreamers.

To what extent have these dreamers drawn their inspiration from our land, waters and built environment—the place where they felt rooted? This is something we may only speculate upon, but there must have been some influence. As the French writer and historian François-René de Chateaubriand stated, "Every man carries with him a world which is composed of all that he has seen and loved, and to which he consistently returns [at least in thought]." Sense of place is partly the memories and emotional meanings associated with a particular landscape and partly the direct inspiration of that landscape as one views it today, whether or not there are past associations. It is also knowing something of the history of a place.

St. Petersburg's uniqueness and sense of place may be described as a vibrant city with an outstanding array of waterfront and other parks, preserves and beaches; a subtropical paradise that celebrates tourism but seeks to diversify its economy to other sectors, including emphasis on marine science; a rich mixture of historic and new architecture; distinctive neighborhoods that have strong neighborhood associations; a metropolis with a big town feel, particularly in the downtown; an abundance of cultural activities; a community where people from all walks of life are welcomed and appreciated; a community proud of its history and traditions but also willing to explore and embrace new ideas and technology; and a community of people who love their city, have sought to make it even better and continue to do so. This is not to say that St. Petersburg does not face challenges. Rather, these are the strengths providing a foundation for meeting those challenges.

Sources used in this chapter include Raymond Arsenault, *St. Petersburg and the Florida Dream: 1888–1950*; City of St. Petersburg, "A City on the Rise…A City of the Arts"; *City of St. Petersburg Comprehensive Plan*; City of St. Petersburg, "Vision 2020"; City of St. Petersburg, "What Defines the Historic Character of St. Petersburg?" City of St. Petersburg website (various); Steven Feld and Keith H. Basso, eds., *Sense of Place*; Kevin Lynch, *What Time Is This Place?*; Will Michaels, "St. Petersburg: A Sense of Place," *Northeast Journal*, 2009; Gary R. Mormino, *Land of Sunshine, State of Dreams: A Social History of Modern Florida*; Pinellas County Planning Department, "Pinellas County Socioeconomic Report," 2004; *St. Petersburg Times*; Scott Taylor Hartzell, *Remembering St. Petersburg*, vol. 2; Rosalie Peck and Jon Wilson, *St. Petersburg's Historic 22nd Street South*; Maria D. Vesperi, *City of Green Benches*; and interview with architects Tim Clemmons and Charles Haung.

Selected Bibliography

For unpublished works and other chapter-specific sources, see the resource notes at the end of each chapter.

Apple, Marty. *Pinstripe Empire: The New York Yankees from Before the Babe to After the Boss*. New York: Bloomsbury, 2012.

Arsenault, Raymond. *St. Petersburg and the Florida Dream: 1888–1950*. Gainesville: University Press of Florida, 1996. Originally published in 1988.

Ayers, R. Wayne. *St. Petersburg: The Sunshine City*. Charleston, SC: Arcadia Publishing, 2001.

———. *Tampa Bay's Gulf Beaches*. Charleston, SC: Arcadia Publishing, 2002.

Baker, Rick. *Mangroves to Major League: A Timeline of St. Petersburg, Florida*. St. Petersburg, FL: Southern Heritage Press, 2000.

———. *The Seamless City*. Washington, D.C.: Regency Publishing, 2011.

Bethell, John A. *Bethell's History of Pinellas Point*. St. Petersburg, FL: Great Outdoors Publishing, 1962. Originally published in 1914.

Betz, Myrtle Scharrer. *Yesterday I Lived in Paradise: The Story of Caladesi Island*. Tampa, FL: University of Tampa, 2009. Originally published in 1984.

Breslauer, Ken. *Historic Sites and Architecture of St. Petersburg, Florida*. Denver, CO: Outskirts Press, 2011.

Brown, Lynne. *Gulfport: A Definitive History*. Charleston, SC: The History Press, 2004.

Brown, Warren. *Florida's Aviation History: The First One Hundred Years*. 2nd ed. Largo, FL: Aero-Medical Consultants, 1994.

Covington, James W. "Babe Ruth and His Record 'Home Run' at Tampa." *Sunshine Tribune: Journal of the Tampa Historical Society* 17 (November 1991).

Davies, R.E.G. *Airlines of the United States Since 1914*. Washington, D.C.: Smithsonian Institution Press, 1972.

Davis, Enoch Douglas. *On the Bethel Trail*. St. Petersburg, FL: Valkyrie Press, 1979.

Deese, A. Wynelle. *St. Petersburg, Florida: A Visual History*. Charleston, SC: The History Press, 2006.

DeLorimier, Finnette Gilbart, and Charles T. deLorimier. *The Saga of Two Sojourners: The Memoirs of Finnette & Chuck deLorimier*. Newark, DE: Bullfrog Publishing, 2000.

De Quesada, A.M. *Baseball in Tampa Bay*. Charleston, SC: Arcadia Publishing, 2000.

Dunn, Hampton. *Yesterday's St. Petersburg*. Miami, FL: E.A. Seeman Publishing, 1973.

Feld, Steven, and Keith H. Basso, eds. *Senses of Place*. Santa Fe, NM: School of American Research Press, 1996.

Fountain, Charles. *Under the March Sun: The Story of Spring Training*. New York: Oxford University Press, 2009.

Fuller, Walter P. *St. Petersburg and Its People*. St. Petersburg, FL: Great Outdoors Publishing Company, 1972.

Gould, Rita Slaght. *Pioneer St. Petersburg*. St. Petersburg, FL: Page Creations, 1987.

Grismer, Karl H. *The Story of St. Petersburg*. St. Petersburg, FL: P.K. Smith, 1948.

Hartzell, Scott Taylor. *Remembering St. Petersburg, Florida*. Vols. 1 and 2. Charleston, SC: The History Press, 2006.

———. *Voices of America: St. Petersburg*. Charleston, SC: Arcadia Publishing, 2002.

Homan, Lynn M., and Thomas Reilly. *Wings Over Florida*. Charleston, SC: Arcadia Publishing Company, 1999.

Hurley, Frank T., Jr. *Pass-a-Grille Vignettes: Times Past, Tales Remembered*. N.p. privately published by Friends of the Gulf Beaches Historical Museum, 1999.

———. *Surf, Sand, & Postcard Sunsets: A History of Pass-a-Grille and the Gulf Beaches*. N.p.: privately printed, 1989. Originally published in 1977.

Jackson, Page S. *St. Petersburg, An Informal History*. St. Petersburg, FL: Great Outdoors Publishing Company, 1962.

Kyle, Gerald, and Garry Chick. "The Social Construction of Sense of Place." *Leisure Sciences* 29 (2007): 209–25.

Lynch, Kevin. *What Time Is This Place?* Cambridge, MA: MIT Press, 1972.

Marth, Del. *St. Petersburg: Once Upon a Time*. St. Petersburg, FL: published by the City of St. Petersburg, [1976].

McCarthy, Kevin M. *Aviation in Florida*. Sarasota, FL: Pineapple Press, 2003.

———. *Baseball in Florida*. Sarasota, FL: Pineapple Press, 1996.

Moffi, Larry, and Jonathan Kronstadt. *Babe Ruth in Florida*. Haverford, PA: Infinity Publishing Company, 2002.

———. *Crossing the Line: Black Major Leaguers, 1947–1959*. Iowa City: University of Iowa Press, 1994.

Montville, Leigh. *The Big Bam: The Life and Times of Babe Ruth*. New York: Doubleday, 2006.

Mormino, Gary R. *Land of Sunshine, State of Dreams: A Social History of Modern Florida*. Gainesville: University Press of Florida, 2005.

Parry, Albert. *Full Steam Ahead!: The Story of Peter Demens*. St. Petersburg, FL: Great Outdoors Publishing Company, 1987.

Peck, Rosalie, and Jon Wilson. *St. Petersburg's Historic African American Neighborhoods*. Charleston, SC: The History Press, 2006.

———. *St. Petersburg's Historic 22nd Street South*. Charleston, SC: The History Press, 2006.

Pederson, Paul. *Build It and They Will Come: The Arrival of the Tampa Bay Devil Rays*. Stuart: Florida Sports Press, 1997.

Pettengill, George W. *The Story of the Florida Railroads*. Jacksonville, FL: Railway and Locomotive Historical Society, 1998. Originally published in 1952.

Pinellas County Department of Environmental Management. *The Weedon Island Story*. Pinellas County Government Publication, 2005.

Reilly, Thomas. *Jannus: An American Flyer*. Gainesville: University of Florida Press, 1997.

Resendez, Andres. *A Land So Strange: The Epic Journey of Cabeza de Vaca*. New York: Basic Books, 2007.

Reynolds, Kelly. *Henry Plant, Pioneer Empire Builder*. Cocoa: Florida Historical Society Press, 2003.

Roberts, Elda M. *The Stubborn Fisherman: A History of the Roberts Family*. Port Aransas, TX: Creighton Publishing, 1970.

Rooks, Sandra W. *St. Petersburg, Florida*. Charleston, SC: Arcadia Publishing, 2003.

Starkey, Jay B. *Things I Remember*. Reprint, Brooksville, FL: Southwest Water Management District, 1980.

Stevenson, R. Bruce. *Visions of Eden*. Columbus: Ohio State University Press, 1997.

Taun, Yi-Fu. *Space and Place: The Perspective of Experience*. Minneapolis: University of Minnesota Press, 2001. Originally published in 1977.

Taylor, Prudy. *The Renaissance Vinoy: St. Petersburg's Crown Jewel*. Virginia Beach, VA: Donning Company, 1999.

Turner, Gregg M. *Railroads of Southwest Florida*. Charleston, SC: Arcadia Publishing, 1999.

Turner, Gregg M., and Seth H. Bramson. *The Plant System of Railroads, Steamships, and Hotels*. Laurays Station, PA: Garrigues House Publishers, 2004.

Vesperi, Maria D. *City of Green Benches: Growing Old in a New Downtown*. Ithaca, NY: Cornell University Press.

Waters, Zack C. "Tampa's Forgotten Defenders the Confederate Commanders of Fort Brooke." *Sunland Tribune: Journal of the Tampa Historical Society* 17 (November 1991).

Wells, Judy Lowe. *C. Perry Snell: His Place in St. Petersburg, Florida History*. N.p.: privately published, 2006.

White, Gay Blair. *The World's First Airline: The St. Petersburg–Tampa Airboat Line*. 2nd ed. Edited by Warren J. Brown. Largo, FL: Aero Medical Consultants, 1984.

Williams, Eugene L. *My Life Story*. N.p.: privately published, 2010.

Young, June Hurley. *The Don Ce-Sar Story*. St. Petersburg, FL: Partnership Press, 1990. Originally published in 1974.

Zazier, Marion. *The Beneficent Blaze: The Story of Major Lew B. Brown*. New York: Pageant Press.1960.

Index

C

G

H

R

S

Y

About the Author

Will Michaels has served as executive director and trustee of the St. Petersburg Museum of History, vice-president of the Carter G. Woodson Museum of African American History, president of St. Petersburg Preservation and co-chair of the Tony Jannus Distinguished Aviation Society and is currently president of the Flight 2014 Planning Board, which is coordinating the celebrations for the centennial of the world's first airline. Community involvements have included service as president of the Council of Neighborhoods and design chair of the St. Petersburg Pier Advisory Task Force. He recently served as a member of the convening group of St. Petersburg Together. Will has a doctorate in anthropology from the University of South Florida and is a recipient of the Anthropology Department's Distinguished Alumnus Award. He is retired from the United States Army Reserve as a lieutenant colonel. A forty-year St. Petersburg resident, he is married to Kathy and has three adult children and four grandchildren.

Other Works by the Author

Published by the St. Petersburg *Northeast Journal*:

"The Snell-Bishop Home: A Marriage of Art and History" (2005)
"Celebrating the 4th of July in St. Petersburg" (2005)
"Our Oldest Neighborhoods" (2006)
"C. Perry Snell" (2006)
"John's Pass—Or Is It Juan's Pass?" (2006)
"Meddlers or Visionaries?: The Woman's Town Improvement Association" (2006)
"The Sunshine School: A State of Happiness" (2006)
"'Florida' Roberts—St. Pete's Most Famous Fisherman" (2007)
"Senator Henry Sayler: Friend of Presidents" (2007)
"The Challenge of Boca Ciega Bay" (2007)
"The Garden Cafeteria & Our Cafeteria Culture" (2007)
"The Detroit: Queen Mother of St. Pete's Hotels" (2007)
"Christmas of Yesteryears" (2007)
"St. Petersburg Conquers World War II" (2007)
"Bill Cooper's 85 Years in St. Pete" (2008)
"Doc Webb: Friend of the Little Guy" (2008)
"Much to Be Thankful For" (2008)
"St. Peter's Cathedral" (2009)
"Boyd Hill Nature Preserve" (2009)
"Dinning in Style: Ralph Graves, Jr." (2010)
"Title to the Pier Challenged" (2010)
"Landscaping the City: Phil Graham, Jr." (2010)
"Winter Home of the Amazing Mets" (2010)
"William Straub's Waterfront Revisited" (2010)
"Jamming With the Best: LeRoy L. Flemmings, Jr." (2010)
"Personalities of the Roaring '20s" (2011)
"Our Forgotten Mayor: Albert T. Blocker" (2011)
"Tony Jannus and the World's First Airline Stamp" (2011)
"Our New Pier—A Sense of Place" (2010)
"Celebrating Old Northeast" (2012)
"Election Times" (2012)

Other:

St. Peter's Cathedral History, 1889–1961

Visit us at
www.historypress.net